天降甘霖，泽披物流先驱者；
恩逢雨露，福惠货代有心人！
God Bestows a Timely Rain,
and Benefits Logistics Vanguards;
God Bestows a Favour,
and Benefits Prepared Freight Forwarders.

天霖宝典

The FORWARD Management Intelligence

天馗 著

文化艺术出版社
Culture and Art Publishing House

图书在版编目（CIP）数据

天霖宝典：汉英对照／天馗著.－北京：文化艺术出版社，
2007.2
ISBN 978-7-5039-3213-7

Ⅰ.天… Ⅱ.天… Ⅲ.企业文化－通俗读物－汉、英
Ⅳ.F270

中国版本图书馆CIP数据核字（2007）第019844号

天霖宝典

著　　者　天馗
责任编辑　董耘
责任校对　崔建文
装帧设计　宝华
插图绘制　王艋　李春明
出版发行　文化艺术出版社
地　　址　北京市朝阳区惠新北里甲1号　　100029
网　　址　www.whyscbs.com
电子邮箱　whysbooks@263.net
电　　话　(010)64813345　64813346（总编室）
　　　　　(010)64813384　64813385（发行部）
经　　销　新华书店
印　　刷　国英印务有限公司
版　　次　2007年2月第1版
　　　　　2007年2月第1次印刷
开　　本　720×960毫米　1/16
印　　张　14.25
字　　数　40千字
书　　号　ISBN 978-7-5039-3213-7/G·628
定　　价　48.00元

目录

序言

　　天降甘霖，泽披物流先驱者；恩逢雨露，福惠货代有心人！

　　自改革开放以后，物流业在中国这片富饶的土地上正如雨后春笋般蓬勃成长，日益壮大，而传统物流业一直被视为不用智慧的粗活。随着时代的进步，多家大型跨国物流企业逐步进驻，在与本土物流业的相互冲击下，已逐渐产生巨大转型，物流业已成为经济发展的血液，成为中华民族再次腾飞的翅膀！

　　本书作者取名"馗"，乃九首合一，是集体意念所在，是福慧与财禄的化身。天馗不是指个人，泛指"天霖国际货运集团"整个团队，是多年来致力开拓中国物流业的集体智慧结晶，体现中国特色的本土物流业与先进的国际物流理念的土洋结合，融会贯通，创新变革！本书从不同的视觉角度，通过形象的表述，结合生动的寓言、漫画及故事，诠释了全新的物流理念及物流业精彩纷呈的管理精粹，再现了天霖人对行业文化的心得与体会，对物流业辉煌前景的信心及孜孜不倦的追求！

　　值"天霖国际货运集团"进军国内物流业十周年之际，谨以此书作为与广大中国市场经济开拓者、广大拟进入中国物流市场的国际物流人士、广大本土物流从业者相互交流的机会。以中国为基础，放眼世界，建立全新的物流管理理念，推动物流业的繁荣昌盛，为国家的富强，民族的振兴贡献一份绵力！内文如有不妥善之处，恭请各界友好、学者指正！

天馗

Preface

God bestows a timely rain, and benefits logistics vanguards; God bestows a favour, and benefitsrepared freight forwarders.

The logistics industry has been mushrooming in China, the fertile divine land on this planet, since the nation started reform and opening up in 1978. Nowadays, the industry in China is no longer what it was in the past, described as one that needed rough work only and without intelligence. As time goes on, a big crowd of foreign multinational logistics operators have edged into the most potential market and competed with the indigenous counterparts, and the indigenous logistics industry has undertaken substantial change, and become the blood for economic growth and the wings for the takeoff of the Chinese people.

The author entitles his book as Kui, which is the incarnation of collectivism, fortune and wealth. Tian Kui is never typical of any individual but a team, and reflects the fruit of collective wisdom FORWARD Group has accumulated since it was dedicated to the local logistics industry, and the combination of the unique Chinese logistic concepts with international logistic concepts. It stands for digestion, absorption, innovation and reform. By introducing vivid fables, cartoons and stories, the author will interpret fire-new logistic concepts and essence of the wonderful management experiences in different ways, present the experience and understandings of the industrial culture, and express the confidence in the promising prospect of and the continuous pursuit of the industry.

With the approach of the tenth anniversary for FORWARD Group's entrance to the China mainland's logistics industry, the author is looking forward to chances to communicating with Chinese market economy vanguards, international logistics executives hoping to enter China, and indigenous logistics operators. FORWARD Group is based in China, but has an international insight. We will do what we can to build brand-new logistic management concepts, advance the logistics industry to prosperity and contribute our own strength to a wealthy and powerful nation and revitalization of the Chinese people. The author hopes friends and scholars will kindly and unselfish correct any improper contents of the book.

Tian Kui

天降甘霖，泽披物流先驱者；
恩逢雨露，福惠货代有心人！
God Bestows a Timely Rain,
and Benefits Logistics Vanguards;
God Bestows a Favour,
and Benefits Prepared Freight Forwarders.

技艺篇

The Chapter on "Artistry"

　　优秀卓越的管理者切忌："工时长、缺效率；下属多、不善用；心过好、聚冗员；怨妇格、常推卸；勤笔耕、忘跟进；死固执、无突破；硬好强、轻善恶；抢邀功、乏内涵；播音嘴、难守秘；少沟通、生嫌隙；白鸽眼、井底娃。"你可对号入座？

　　An excellent manager shall strain every nerve to avoid long-time inefficient work, bad use of subordinates, kind-hearted recruitment of too many employees, and regular transfer of his work to others. He had better try every effort to make breakthrough rather than adhere to regular patterns, distinguish between goodwill and hostility rather than firmly stick to his own opinions, and cultivate his self-restraint rather than eagerly rush to ask for rewards. He shall keep secrets, communicate with subordinates regularly and persist in learning. Have you had done all of these well?

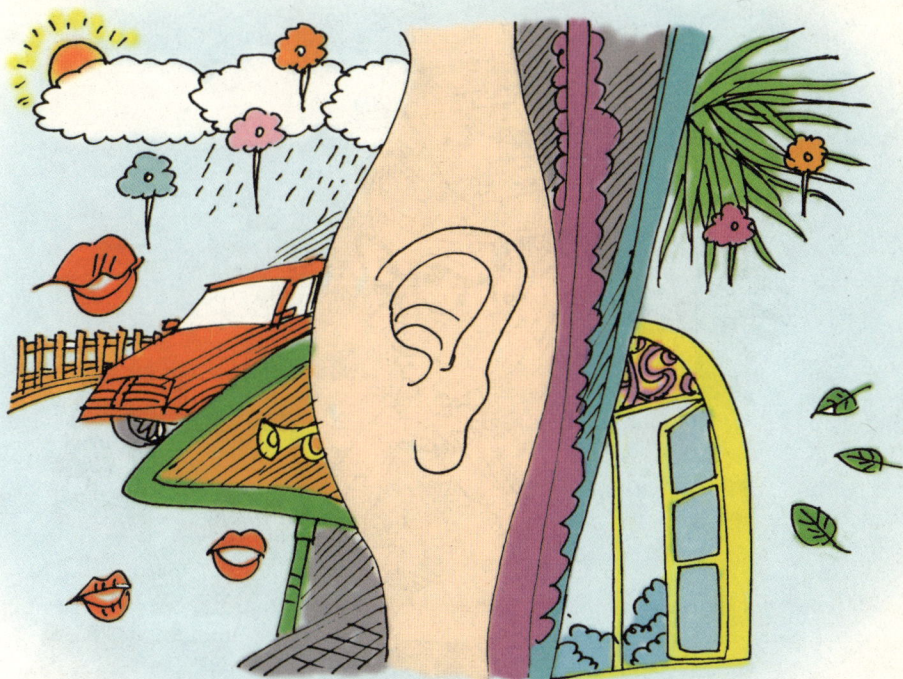

　　一个精明的管理者用眼睛来做事、成事、分析对错；过于用耳朵来听纳下属工作失误的解释，则令其恶化、退步，更令自己亦进步不了！"巧合"两字不存在工作错误里！请酌情把耳朵藏好。

A smart manager makes decision and distinguishes subordinates' lies by his or her own eyes, not by his or her ears. Depending too much on what you hear will mislead your judgment, or even make your management exacerbated. Never speak lightly "I accept it". Never believe that coincidence is the only reason for any fault in work. Is there any person who doesn't know how to dodge and cover his or her mistakes? So please cover your ears carefully to free from possible misleading.

沟通是学问！没有永远理解能力差的下属，只有表达能力有限的上级，同样误事！英明的主管于沟通过程中需学习"聆听——思考——决策——表达"，耐心听取你下属的话，透过思考、分析才能准确地作决定！急就章的做法肯定走冤枉路！除非你自问已升华至举一反三之境地。

Communication is quite an art! There is no subordinate who can't understand what you said, but only you sometimes can't express yourself clearly. A smart leader performs well up in listening, thinking, decision making and expressing precisely, during communication. Only after listening carefully, thinking and analyzing deeply, then you can have good decision made. Decision in rash will always cost you more than your expectation.

4

　　当你感觉工作压力大时，试深呼吸，对着镜子笑、笑、笑；当你感觉闲着没活干，也许你真的效率高，也许你已把过往的工作积压不顾，断层脱钩了！学会每天"温故知新"规律处事啊！

　　When you feel mounting pressure from your work, try to have a deep breath and smile to yourself in front the mirror. When you feel free, you may enjoy a high efficiency in doing your work or have neglected the work your have not done and make these unfinished work not well connected! Just review what you have learned every day and follow regular patterns to do things right.

一个称职（不奢望超卓）的经理人必须具备"经"营及管"理"技巧！不难，牢记四大要诀："量化"问题后对症下药，"沟通"及时，对难题"不妥协"，让各下属"神往"于政策里……切勿形成"上梁不正下梁歪"，令下属有样学样，进步不了！

A competent manager must have operating and management skills! He shall always remember four recipes, that is to say, to work out solutions after quantifying problems, ensure immediate communications with others, never flinch in the face of hard problems and to develop the empathy between the company and subordinates . Besides, he shall absolutely not set bad examples for his subordinates!

　　"强化礼貌及服务意识"已推行多月，效果如何仍待评估；但作为主管的你必须以身作则，贯彻推行！其身不正者定难以让新政普及下属！最终自招苦果！

　　The strategy of intensifying employees' awareness of services manners has been promoted for several months, and the effect is still pending evaluation! As FORWARD manager, you shall take the lead in implementing this strategy! If you can't behave yourself, it will be hard for you to popularize this strategy among your subordinates and finally, you may have no choice but to wait for the bad results!

　　天霖人皆是"风险管理人"，亦同样为"财会监控者"：严控你部开销、经营情况、杜灭无理支出、量化思维、寻隙节约！必须实事求是，报喜"先"报忧，做到"全民皆财控、你我齐表功"。

　　Every FORWARD manager shall be risk-controller as well as financial controller, responsible for controlling the spending, operation and cost saving within their department! They shall also seek truth from facts, dig deep into the records to find out hidden difficulties, and possess of the common hope of seeking success in controlling financial costs.

治乱世用重典，管用！对冥顽不灵的员工、对加速扭转管理制度的漏弊，下手狠点，同样管用！疼过才知疼、知改！

Severe punishment is very useful for regulating troubled times! It also works for managing employees with poor understanding and quickening the completion and perfection of the existing management system. Only after employees feel pains from severe punishment, they will clearly know they should take immediate steps to correct mistakes, especially in China.

　　"时间就是金钱"这句耳熟能详的话一点不假！能够身处天霖的发展巨轮内就得掌握时间，积极计划每天、每月、每年的工作与前程，丰盛人生唾手可得！该做"好"的工作不因时间失控而消失，只会积压更多。管不好时间亦管不好人！

　　The common saying that "Time is money" is really true! Every participant in the company's development shall make good use of time and make plans and set targets for their work every day, every month and every year. In this way, it will be easier for the participant to enjoy a bright career. Unfinished work will not accomplish automatically because of your waste of time, but to get together. Poor management of time just means poor management of people!

时间管理关键是酌情下放工作及权力、明确目标及完工前后的监督……乃律己律人、量材为用之道；不善文笔不成文秘，不懂风险不审合同、不负责任绝不能用！

The key to time management is to transfer work and rights to the lower level in accordance with actual circumstances, define the target and tighten the surveillance. A wise manager shall blame himself as he would blame others and give subordinates work suited to their abilities. He shall not designate to those who do not adept at writing to serve as secretary or ask those who do not know risks to review contracts. He absolutely can't recruit irresponsible people, notwithstanding how capable they are!

　　"处惊不变"乃反应慢、无应急方案的拙劣反映；"处变不惊"感觉稍好但仍欠不足，应先把全局透彻掌握后，制订"针对性"方案才可"挥洒自如、运筹帷幄"！要成事必须部署周详，切勿冒尖瞎冲。

　　"Staying unscared in the face of stock" is actually the reflection of slow reaction and the absence of solutions in response to emergence. "Staying calm in the face of upheaval"seems to be better while is not so sufficient. A wise manager shall bring forward solutions after he gets the overall situation. Only in this way, he can act freely and plan strategies within a command tent! He shall make good arrangement and shall absolutely not rush blindly if he wants to succeed in doing things.

　　管理者常犯的错误就是过于依赖书面报告；久之，则官僚歪风自成、内部问题越显恶劣！书面"报告"必须有，但管理水平高下仍看最终结果！

　　A common fault managers frequently make is that they tend to depend too much on what writing reports state. This may lead to red-tapism and serious internal chaos after a long period of time. The writing reports are necessary, while the management shall still be judged from the final results!

　　身为主管必须设定内部沟通机制，对本部的一切异常情况掌握清楚后牵头处理。已存在的问题不因你的忽略而变得好转，该完成的工作不因你的耽搁而自动完成。预防胜于治疗，治疗胜于不治疗。

　　The FORWARD manager shall formulate internal communication mechanism and lead other subordinates to resolve abnormal situations after he acquires all situations thoroughly. Existing problems will not turn better because of your neglance. And the unfinished work will not automatically accomplish because of your delay. The manager had better take precaution rather than wait to receive a consequent treatment and had better accept treatment other than give a refusal.

　　企业管理及发展必须有完善的流程、模式才可生生不息。惟主管往往因不认知真正的流程而自乱步伐，亦乱了他人步伐，结果全乱套了，天天忙于善后与补救，整体哪会进步？不在乎人数多寡，只在乎性格手法！

　　The management and development of an enterprise shall follow perfect procedures and patterns. How can the enterprise make headway, if the supervisor is busy dealing with problems every day because of his disobedience such procedures and patterns? Please do not care too much how many employees you have. Just care about their characteristics and ways for treating problems!

　　天霖人因蜕变而美丽！谨记"以科学战胜官僚；以客观摧毁武断；以精细取代浮夸"！

　　Changes make FORWARD staff more bright. Always bear it in mind to defeat bureaucracy with science, to overcome subjectiveness with objectiveness, and supercede inaccuracy with precision.

成事不全靠双手。先用"心"出发，再用"脑"，才到"手"。心正自然观念正，手法正确少走弯路。哪怕不百分之百成功亦不至太难看。

Try to succeed not only with your hands! Start with your heart, then use your brains, and finally do it with your hands. A kind heart naturally leads to correct ideas, lawful methods and right way. With these, you will not lose your face even if you don't make it completely!

　　工作上的谬误多因"不懂装懂及一知半解";知多点自会少错点。厚颜谦逊、不耻下问管用!资深者理应耐心"帮带",认真传授;多带出"水平人"更显自身"本事大"!私心作祟,则人型低俗!

　　Mistakes in work usually result from limited knowledge and smatter. The more you know, the less mistakes you will make. Be modest and ready to learn from others, even from the younger and inferior! Veteran predecessors shall be patient to teach others and the success in helping others achieve advancement can better reflect your talent! Any selfishness will damage your image!

　　未"彻底"完成的工作仍是"未完成"。砌词搪塞、虎头虫尾、做表面功夫者，足证管理意识有误，自身及团队均难成大器！"忙与忘"乃借口及恶习！

　　Any incompletely completed work still remains uncomplete. To avoid responsibility, to start well but end bad, and to speak louder than actions prove nothing but wrong sense of the manager. Any manager of this kind will never lead himself and the team to success. Busy and forget is an excuse and bad habit.

重原则不是硬坚持，应择善固执；劳苦不一定功高，应以自身的业绩作衡量。优胜劣汰，乃先天与后天品性、手法的结合，与人无忧！

Sticking to principles is never blind-minded adhesion to everything, but to good things only. Hard work does not necessarily lead to big merit, but depends on performance. Success or failure is the result from the combination of endowment and acquired quality and methodology, and does not have anything to do with others.

　　没有解决不了的工作难题,只有不懂解决难题或手法谬误的主管! 不妨主动与同僚、上级或本部人员磋商、请教、咨询、研讨对策,集思广益。只怕自尊心作祟、自以为是或惯性处事假大空而已!

　　There is no hard problem that can not be solved! There are only supervisors who do not know how to settle the problem or do not have good solutions! Please actively negotiate and consult with your colleagues, higher-level managers or subordinates for drawing upon all useful opinions and working out countermeasures! We are afraid of nothing, but handling affairs with overstrong self-esteem, self-righteousness or previous experience!

工作上的问题解决不了，事出有因："砌词搪塞永不言错、勇于认错但无能为力、点到即止乏贯彻跟进。"此乃人性三大丑，是成败关键，直接影响绩效、领军及企业发展！

If problems in work cannot be settled, there must be some reasons! Strong adherence to rightness with excuses, disability despite the courage to acknowledge faults, and no awareness of implementation and following, are the three kinds of human nature, directly affect FORWARD's performance, management and development!

考核制度

完善的绩效考核制度乃现今管理手法的最高境界，是汰弱留强、逼使各级人员进步的有力工具。只许成功，不许失败！它犹如宏观调控结合微观整改，企业才得以更新壮大。挡路者一定出局，不须惋惜！阵痛过后见金光！

Performance appraisal system is the tiptop state of the current management ways and a powerful weapon to wash out weaker ones and retain stronger ones and to urge various levels of employees to improve themselves! Only success, other than any failure, is allowed! Just as the combination of macro control and micro restructuring, it enables enterprises to become much stronger. The disturbed must be eliminated. Please do no feel sorry for this! They may find out their true value finally!

　　沟通过程中的谬误或抓不住对方的中心思想时，多因自我意识重、保护欲强、固步自封的条件反射而致。你宁一辈子当刺猬？

Misunderstandings or failure to get main ides during the communication always result from overstrong self-awareness, self-protection or conditioned reflex of self-limitation. Will you be content to behave just like a hedgehog in your whole life?

　　人性本惰！纸上谈兵、滞后拖延何其多！懂自我鞭策者必成大器；反之，必须强行对己、对下属施压才见进步。压力下见成果堪回味！经一事，长一智，管理经验与手法乃日积月累，无浑然天成的。

　　Human beings are naturally lazy! Too many people are engaging in idle theorizing, lagging or lingering. The self-motivated are bound to succeed; whereas, only put the manager and its subordinates under pressure, can some advancement be made. Results achieved under pressure are always unforgettable! Experience is the mother of wisdom! Management experience is always accumulated and naturally formed over a long period.

何谓称职？粗心者不能担任财会、缺流程认知者管不好操作、苟且含糊者当不成行政、轻率怠惰者把不住保卫、欠机灵敏锐者做不成销售、不善平衡者演不活人资、计较迂腐者理不顺关务。用人必先知人、量材应先量己！

What's competence? The careless are not competent for finance or accounting, the insensitive to process are not qualified for operation, the perfunctory are not suitable for administrative affairs, the lazy don't do well as guards, the blunt-minded don't sell well. Still, those unable to handle interpersonal relations are not eligible for human resources, and those incapable to adjust to changing situations are not suitable for public relations. Know your men well before using them, and know yourself well before knowing others!

越高层就越要懂得分配资源、善用人力；一篮子往自己肩上扛肯定顾此失彼、吃力不讨好！处事水平高下立判。

The higher-level post you take, the better you shall understand how to allocate resources! If you shoulder too much responsibility, your back will break! And treatment with responsibility against your position immediately reveals your management level.

　　联欢晚会的氛围易让人陶醉。杯酒当歌已过，就更须以公平、不徇私手法带领员工共创繁荣。"大公无私"知易行难，越公正就越得民心！

　　People always feel intoxicated at evening parties. After hobnobbing, a wise manager shall lead its subordinates to create prosperity with more fair mind and more unselfish heart. To be selfless, he shall pick up harder issues in spite of the awareness of easier ones. The more he behaves fairly, the more morale he will win!

　　在天霖的管理模式内一定要力求公平、公私分明、用人唯材才有长远发展空间，而结合中国特色的裙带户只在对等条件下才显优势，不足以构筑成特种"白蚁穴"来毁灭无私的团队精神！

The FORWARD's management mode must pursue fairness, clear-cut distinction between public and private affairs, appropriate use of talents and creation of long-term growth space for them. China-specific nepotism shows its advantages under the same conditions, and should never destroy the unselfish teamwork spirit.

精明的主管必须驾驭全局、发挥下属所长齐突破、创佳绩；而不是盲从附和；心软耳轻，被下属的陋习牵引而致自失方寸，共同倒退！

A wise supervisor shall be able to command the overall situation and draw upon subordinates' advantages to make breakthrough and produce excellent results! He shall not blindly follow or go along with others. If he is warmhearted or tend to believe others, he may lose his calmness and lag behind together with his subordinates, once affected by his subordinates' weaknesses.

天降甘霖，泽披物流先驱者；
恩逢雨露，福惠货代有心人！
God Bestows a Timely Rain,
and Benefits Logistics Vanguards;
God Bestows a Favour,
and Benefits Prepared Freight Forwarders.

风险篇

The Chapter on "Risk Controls"

　　成熟的管理者从不轻视新任务。风险意识薄弱源于惯性的积非成是、因循怠慢陋习所致！凡事越周详策划则越无后顾之忧！黄金机会一纵即逝，未必每次有扭转余地。轻率不了啊！

　　A mature manager never neglects new tasks. Weak consciousness of risks results from longtime bad habit of treating the wrong as the right and laziness. The more carefully you make a prior plan, the fewer cares you will have. A valuable opportunity never waits! You may not have leeway to recapture the lost opportunity every time. Never be careless!

　　风险管理意识就是要敏锐、洞察、分析，不轻易相信"表面证据"，否则天天灭火而不是防火！必须同时对相关规条、流程及操作要求了解才不致被假相误导！任何负面的人、物、事皆可"燎原"！

　　To have risk management consciousness is just to keep keen, observe carefully and analyze. Never believe phenomenal evidences easily, or you will have to put out fires rather than take all reasonable precautions every day. Also familiarize yourself with relevant policies, procedures and rules so that you will not be misled by misleading facts. Any negative person, material and affair may spread like wildfire.

　　内部不团结肯定不可取。团队不和肯定令信息滞后、固步自封、错失商机，这样迟早拖垮业绩、拖垮自己！

Internal disharmony is never good in any way. A disharmonizing team is definite to have out-of-date information, lose heart to progress and miss commercial opportunities. Such a team will end up no where but phase out and spoil the overall performance.

　　风险管理在于培育危机意识，乃"预防胜于补救"；抢占市场在于内外配合、团结促销，乃"主动压倒一切"。被动而又无改进者必将出局！

　　Risk management is based on cultivation of risk consciousness, namely, prevention is better than cure. To snatch the market relies on good teamwork and united marketing, namely, initiative comes first! Those unwilling to take initiatives and improve are definite to be phased out.

　　风险管理是一场持久耐力战！必须坚持、认真、彻底、责任到人。丝毫苟且、放松不得！管理者要成功、成材必须活在风险评估里，对服务质量要求亦然；遇不可抗力事故亦应积极扭转劣势，输少算赢，勿轻言投降！

　　Risk management requires endurance and perseverance. It involves adhesion, earnestness, completeness and allocation of responsibility to each person. Never be careless. A manager has to live with risk evaluation, if he wishes to succeed. This principle applies to service quality as well. Even in the case of force majeure, you will have to try your best efforts to turn around the inferior position. Lose less is succeed, and never give up easily.

　　重点工作上的连番疏忽、失误与犯险，真是凑巧？越高层就越不应相信"凑巧"！也许是上级错误评估形势或下属能力有限！反正是后悔莫及，再不培育危机管理意识，危险呀！

　　Negligence, mistakes and dangers frequently occur to important work. All are coincidences? The higher position you take, the firmer you should refuse to accept coincidences. Maybe your superior has misjudged the situation, or your inferior has inadequate ability. However, complaints will make up for nothing, no matter how many they are. Still neglect cultivation of risk management consciousness? It is too dangerous!

一子错，未必每次全盘皆输；但肯定产生连带的、连贯的影响，需花翻倍的额外精力才可调改。做人处事、判断出策、分析定论亦然！错而即改绝对比一错再错、永不悔改强！

A single mistake will not cost you everything, but definitely bring consequent negative effects, and you will have to double your efforts to correct. This also applies to your conduct, handling affairs, judgment, decision making, analysis, and conclusion. It is better to correct after making mistakes than repeating them and refusing to correct.

　　书呆子以理论概括一切，实则"闭门造马"；有冲劲者只向前冲，忽视周边人物事或竞争者的动态，实则是"开门撞山"。管理水平与销售技巧必须有"招"，否则一定是假大空！

　　A bookworm generalizes everything with theory, without considering diverse conditions. Aggressive people just press ahead and neglect the development of surrounding people, matters and rivals, just to be terribly hit by the reality. Management level and sales skills require methods and techniques, and otherwise they are just void, false and fruitless.

　　"诚信忠义"乃处世之源，"公平执法"乃管理之本，"不知道"是拙劣管理者对上对下的一贯手法，是对内对外乏监督的表现！姑息一人等同牺牲大众，没完没了！

　　Honesty, credit, loyalty and justice are the root to behave oneself. Fair reinforcement of laws is the base for management, "No Idea" is always the trick of an inferior manager to avoid responsibility, and this is the result of insufficient supervision. To appease one person is equal to sacrifice the public, and negative consequences will never end.

　　工作会议无疑是传达政策与寻求方案的必须品！解决问题应从"防范"起，而防范始于"认真监督"！繁忙时段易见漏弊、空闲时段易招风险。管理者惯性闭门造车或切实作现场督导是区分成败的关键。拿捏准自然问题消。

　　Working conferences are required to make policies known and seek solutions. Problem settlement should start with prevention, while prevention should begin with earnest supervision. Busy period is prone to incur errors and omissions whereas the idle period is prone to incur risks. How a manager behaves is essential to determine the result: A manager turning a blind eye to the reality will lead to failure, while an industrious manager devoted to on-sites supervision will lead to success. Accurately probe the hazard, and you will naturally prevent the problem from happening.

天霖企管文化衍生的MLS经理人评定考核结果已定。得高分者莫喜，既得人和就必须有优秀的业绩衬托才显完美；失分者莫悲，丢了人和还能补救、纠正，只怕连业绩也泡汤！又是自我反思的时候了！

The FORWARD's MLS (Management Leadership Survey) have concluded, and the results have come out. Don't get overexcited on a high score. Broad support is made perfect only with outstanding performance. Don't get depressed on a low score, because you still have chances to correct and come back. It is the time again for you to turn over to think.

市场瞬息万变，管理及处事手法忌"一本书读到老"，必须按既定任务的最终目标来权衡轻重，做到"缓急有序、快慢有度"，切忌颠倒处事！

To seize the changing market, the manager must adapt himself and his way to behave to changing conditions. Tasks must be weighted in line with the ultimate objective. Always remember to distinct tasks by importance and emergency, and always avoid handling them vice versa.

天降甘霖，泽披物流先驱者；
恩逢雨露，福惠货代有心人！
God Bestows a Timely Rain,
and Benefits Logistics Vanguards;
God Bestows a Favour,
and Benefits Prepared Freight Forwarders.

故事篇

The Chapter on "Allegory"

　　天勤国值蜕变期，上下一心各有想法：材德兼备及有德无材者皆磨刀霍霍欲大展身手，自我改造，为打造繁荣昌盛的国度而努力；其余官阶或沉不住气、或执迷不悟、或心胸狭隘、计较，最终因无缘分享天勤国的丰硕果实而引以为憾！

　　During the transformation period, every member of the FORWARD Kingdom has their own ideas: the talented with both ability and political integrity or only ability are eager to give full play to their abilities, improve themselves and make contribution to the kingdom's well-off; of other officials, some lose composure, some obstinately stick to a wrong course and some are narrow-minded. They all feel regrettable finally, as they destroy their chance to share the Kingdom's success!

　　天勤国帅将同心，急于开疆辟土，大事扩军，惟忽略了认真评估兵种的强弱、心态而错配！精兵制无法实施，反而凭自我意识的盲目扩军致令"军饷增加、粮草不继"！为将者有执迷不悔亦有痛定思痛，最终事倍功半，苦战连场，惨不忍睹！

　　When FORWARD's generals and commanders, with one heart, are eager to expand the realm, they expand arms while forget evaluating the strength and mind of different arms of services and wrongly mix them together! Arms reduction can't be implemented, and their blind arms expansion correspondingly leads to the increase of military spending and provisions! Some generals still stick to the wrong course, and some recall the painful experience. They finally get half the result with twice the effort and struggle hard on the battlefield while the results are too horrible to look!

天勤国向律己律人、纲纪严明，以大治为目标！宁牺牲小我，莫蹈昏庸者覆辙：杨门忠烈毁于潘氏；岳家贤仁灭于秦奸！最终民生不振，甘尽苦来！天勤国众将必须身先士卒，勤练杨岳之军才可屡战屡胜；残兵弱将必败无疑！

The FORWARD Kingdom formulates strict disciplines for itself and others to follow and regards the general law and order as its target! It prefers to make a small sacrifice rather than allow any fatuous ruler to track an overturned cart. The loyal Yang family were destroyed by the wicked Pan colt and the Yue family were damaged by the Qin colt. The people eked out a miserable livelihood! In order to succeed in every battle, FORWARD's Generals and commanders have to charge at the head of their soldiers and try every effort to train the arms of the Yang and Yue families. Handicapped warriors and incompetent commanders will fail without question!

天勤国略有基础，帅将上下心态各异：有勤于政务但疏于监管，令其政绩窒碍不前；有开疆辟土但后继无人，令其疲于奔命；有养尊处优、疏于职守又自以为是，令其原地封吏再无寸进；有纵情荣辱、冒进出疆，令其前功尽废！天勤国众将亟需"悟"了，以制衡邻国虎视眈眈之势！

The FORWARD Kingdom has some foundation. Generals and commanders have different minds. Some, attending to governmental affairs while neglecting supervision, don't make any achievement in their posts; some is weighed down with the territorial expansion, as they have no inheritors; Some, living in clover, neglecting of their duty and considering themselves always right, also make no headway in their posts; and some, indulging in honors and rashly heading for the outside of boundary, gain nothing but failure! The masses shall wake up and strive to beat down the thriving threat from neighboring countries!

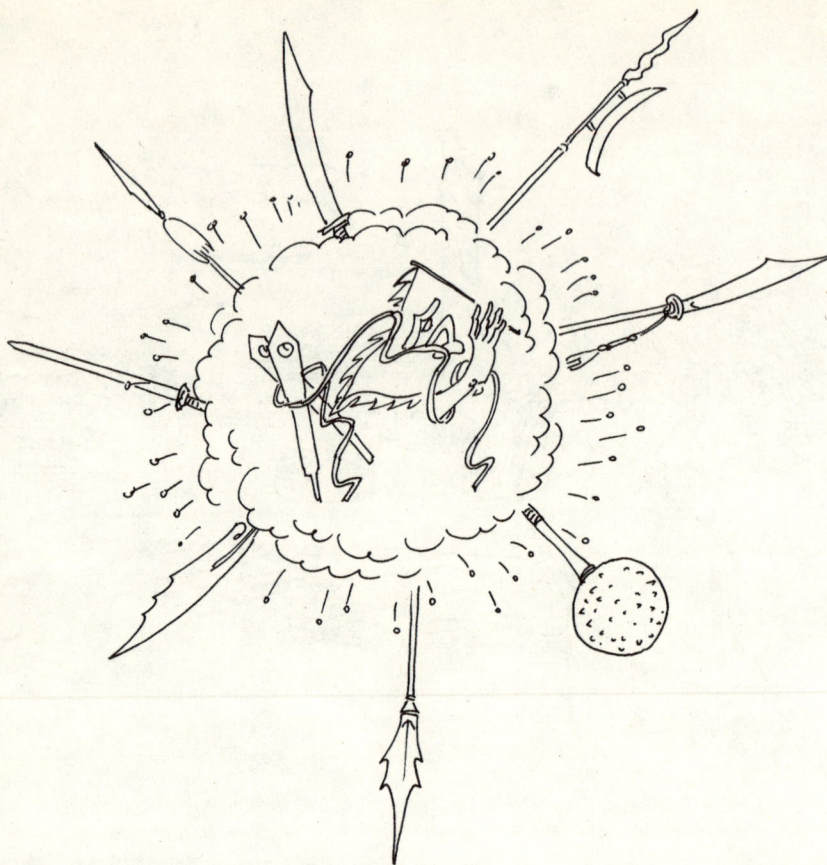

　　天勤国下设吏、户、礼、兵、刑、工、卫、关八部统称"天勤八部"各施司职、环环相扣。后因所属帅将治军失误、加上判断失准致令战事受阻，连番失利！要扭改战果就得摒弃门户之见，共商良策才得以取胜，否则，一部错，八部难以幸存！

The FORWARD Kingdom has the ministries of personnel, revenue, rites, war, justice, public works, safeguard and foreign affairs to take up their respective responsibilities. Later, generals and commanders successively failed in several battles for their worse regulation of the arms and inaccurate judgment of the situation! They soon found out that the sectarian bias shall be thrown away to reverse the war results and these ministries shall jointly discuss about the decision-making to achieve a success, otherwise, it will hard for these eight ministries to survive, if one ministry makes wrong decision.

　　天勤国针对时局、评估全国利弊"坚决改革"、全面推行"全民绩效赏罚法案"！成败取决于"天勤八部"一众帅将对此役之投入与力度！冥顽不配合者或领军水平不足者将酌情被判斩立决！轻视新政者将后悔莫及。

　　In view of the political situation and the evaluation of advantages and disadvantages of the Kingdom, FORWARD starts a reform and promotes a National Performance Appraisal System! Whether it will succeed or not is just up to efforts and strength all generals and commanders of these eight ministries will put into this battle! The disturbed or incompetent leaders will be judged or beheaded in accordance with actual circumstances! Those looking down on the new policies will find it too late for regrets.

伴君也许如伴虎，可虎毒绝不食子：视乎君、臣、帅、将间的默契与心态而已。一统天下前的狐朋狗党必先清除才得以大治，变质变节者与大局脱钩，纵有汗马功劳亦难以立足。持久稳定的局面才是君臣百姓专享荣华之时。

To accompany the emperor may be as dangerous as to accompany a tiger! Vicious as a tigress can be, she never eats her own cubs. It depends on the relation and harmony among the emperor, its officials, generals and commanders. The so-called friends before the king took the sovereinty must be cleared to achieve the general law and order. Corrupted officials don't comply with the general situation and should also be cleared out even if they have made significant contributions to the sovereinty. Only with a permanently stable society, the rulers and the mass can live without cares.

　　天勤国臣民过于沉醉安逸，令朝纲滞后不振，内忧外患重现；亟需群起"治心自灭"才得以重获曙光！灭奸念、诛怠惰、戒拖延、弃官僚。周年复始、孜孜不倦地自我灭魔乃惟一捷径！

　　The FORWARD's rulers and mass are too indulgent in coziness and neglect of the update of the general law and order. The kingdom is again brought in the face of domestic strife and foreign aggression. It can't regain the resplendence unless it urgently eliminates revolting thoughts. It has to kill evil and lazy, prevent against any delay and abandon bureaucracy. The persevering elimination of revolting thoughts is the only short cut!

天降甘霖，泽披物流先驱者；
恩逢雨露，福惠货代有心人！
God Bestows a Timely Rain,
and Benefits Logistics Vanguards;
God Bestows a Favour,
and Benefits Prepared Freight Forwarders.

帅将篇

The Chapter on "Supreme Commander"

带兵取胜之道在于领兵之法：忠诚是关键，但诚信未必成大器、忠心未必全中用！得看领兵者量材为用、取长补短、明确责任，更重要是督导与扶携，共同进步；反之，互相拖垮乃迟早事！

The way to lead arms is the key to victory. Loyalty is crucial while isn't bound for success. Not all loyal people are competent! Leaders shall use personnel according to their abilities, encourage the personnel to learn from other's strong points to offset their own weakness and clearly point out responsibilities for them. More importantly, they shall supervise and support the personnel to improve with them. Otherwise, it is just a matter of time before they collapse.

　　一个遇事只会砌词搪塞、顾左右而言他的主管谈不上高明，是自己骗自己而已！这种苟且侥幸心态、肤浅无知手法者别说是民企，更别说是天霖，走到哪儿也站不住脚。作为上级的你，仍坚持纵容下去？

　　The general who always stalls him off with a vague answer can't be said to be really wise and is only cheating himself. Every country doesn't welcome such perfunctory and aleatory thinking and superficial and empty-headed way for treating problems. It is actually unacceptable anywhere, let alone FORWARD. As an emperor, will you still indulge this?

　　"管人与被管"是一门艺术与学问！当你面对员工流失率大、工作不达标，或上级多次介入时，先行自我检讨管治手法。懂突破求变就是福气；瞎坚持者肯定晦气！

　　"To be in charge of or in the charge of others" is really an art as well as a science! When you are annoyed with severe staff drainage, the failure to meet your target or higher-lever managers' frequent intervention in your work, please review your management techniques first. The efforts to make breakthroughs or changes will bring you good luck; while adherence to your ways will surely bring you bad luck!

　　工作路上充满机遇与压力！当你承受上级批评时，先别压抑、辩解。精明的管理者不轻易无的放矢，反而是给你机会反思、纠正手法！是难受、是挫败、是不甘……亦是锻炼你踏上成功舞台的前奏！

　　There are opportunities as well as pressures during your work! When you are criticized by higher-level managers, please don't try to defend yourself or feel depressed. A wise manager will not criticize its subordinates without an aim, otherwise, they always give them a chance to think over and correct! You may feel sad, frustrated or unreconciled, while it is also the prelude to your step onto the success stage!

糊涂无能或自以为是的上级所做的决策多半是耽误事，最终引火烧身！精明的上级让你做的事一定有其用意，无法奉行自然延误总体战略步署，最终结果一致！

The decisions made by woozy, talentless or self-righteous managers always delay the work and draw fire against themselves! A wise manager has his own intention, if he asks you to finish an assignment. If the assignment can't be accomplished, it naturally delays the execution of the overall strategy and the whole work!

　　好的将领须有周全的战略部署才能克敌制胜；周全的战略亦须一众将领参谋才能驾驭兵种、灵活调动，一举得天下。沙场上无奇迹可言！

　　A good leader can't defeat the enemy or win the battle if he hasn't a thorough strategy. With the thorough strategy, a commander and a brainman are needed to manoeuvre arms of services flexibly to conquer the world at one blow. There is no miracle on the battlefield!

上级的授权乃信任及对下属判断力的肯定！是机会亦是考验。轻重失据自然权力回收！

Managers' authorization reflects their trust on subordinates and their affirmation of subordinates' judgment! It is an opportunity as well as a challenge. If they feel any loss of reliance, they may withdraw such authorization. This is reality!

对人对事"姑"且"放"松，肯定有不停"息"的问题、直接"纵"容下属屡错屡犯！"姑息"与"放纵"注定失败！怀柔、高压手法总比瞻前"缺"后强！身为下属者反思了，你乐意上级永为你担当？争气吧！

If you tentatively forgive your subordinates for their faults, more problems will arise continuously, and other subordinates will repeat their faults! Indulgence certainly leads to failure! The placatory or high-pressure methods are better than over-cautious and indecisive ways! Will these subordinates be willing to let you take upon the consequences for them forever, if they think over? They may try to bring credit to themselves.

超级领导：用有限资源创无限市场，不断更新、开发，抢在头！高级领导：用有限资源维护既有市场，力保不失！一般领导：迁就资源局部放弃市场，于根基未稳时无疑慢性自杀！低级领导：不断令冗员重叠、将无能、兵不力，易招灭亡！

An excellent leader uses limited resources to create the infinite market, never stop updating and developing, and always take the lead! A senior leader uses limited resources to maintain the existing market and try every effort to protect the foothold! A common leader cares too much about resources and abandons part of the market. It always destroys the company at its earlier stage! An inferior leader always recruits too many employees for overlapped work and tends to destroy the company!

强将麾下无弱兵：当你自认强但手下副将战斗力有限时，往往把战果拱手让敌方；这谈不上强，顶多是小地域阵地小将领而已，也许连一个伙头兵也谈不上！

A strong commander has no weak soldiers under its flag. If he believes himself powerful and the second in command is relatively weaker, he will always surrender the success to enemies submissively. He can't be deemed to be powerful and at best be a small commander for a small territory or a small position or even can't be said to be an army cook.

妇人未必皆仁,匹夫未必都勇！为将者必须权衡轻重：妇人之仁与匹夫之勇同样贻误军机、同样坏事！

Not all women are kind, and not all reckless people are brave. A general must bear it in mind that womanish kindness and thoughtless courage are both dangerous, and may cost the rare precious opportunity to win a war.

　　战火正酣，帅将之间的沟通绝不能松懈！"将在外，军令有所不受"，只适用于个别特殊情况，并不构筑为自身的防弹墙，除非强将手下真无弱兵，可运筹帷幄，克敌制胜于千里之外。

　　Communications between the marshal and general shall never be relaxed when a furious battle is going on. Only in very few cases, a general can refuse the order from the marshal. However, this shall never become an excuse in any case unless the general really owns intelligent and courageous soldiers and prominent strategies and tactics, and win a battle without command from the marshal.

帅将之间乃唇齿关系。为帅者应掌握轻重、酌情恩恤下属，以大局为重；为将者应不卑不亢，以力争及不违总体目标为大任。事出必有因，试互处对方立场考虑问题必有新体会！

Marshal and general are mutually dependent. A marshal should distinguish affairs by importance, appropriately favor and forgive his general, and stress importance of the overall situation. In contrast, a general should be neither humble nor arrogant, and make it his chief obligation to comply with and achieve the overall target. No fire, no smoke. The marshal and general should exchange their positions in investigating the cause after an accident, and will surely have new understandings.

　　智、勇、勤兼备者，乃国之栋梁、帅之翘楚；存智、勇而欠勤者，败象纷呈；故勤乃智、勇之源，克敌制胜、剿灭心魔之本！天道酬勤弃惰。

　　Intelligence, courage and diligence make a person the pillar of the country and outstanding marshal, while intelligence and courage in the absence of diligence make a person an unqualified leader. Therefore, diligence is the mother of intelligence and courage, and the basis to win victories and defeat mental evils. God favors the diligent and abandons lazy.

没有不成事的，只有不负责任的将；没有错配的，只有不懂调兵遣将、姑息纵容又手法粗劣的帅。为将不成是混账，封帅无能反类兵！不战而败！

There are no generals who are too incapable to succeed, there are only generals who are irresponsible. There are no marshals who are wrongly appointed, there are only marshals who have no idea how to use his men, indulge his men and inferior tricks. An incompetent general just spoils the matter, and an incapable marshal leads his men to misfortune.

强将手下无弱兵；慈将手下难成材；混将手下乱纲纪。有样学样，责人先责己！当你自命付出最多、最忠诚但多次吃力不讨好又无战果时，乃综合领军能力不足的反映！坚持错误者只会越陷越深，旁人欲帮无从！

A strong general leads no weak troops, an unduly kind general creates no competent troops, and an unqualified general just undermines the discipline and order: The example set by a general is always followed by his troops, and a general should blame himself before blaming others. If you consider yourself the most industrious and loyal, and you have made great pains without corresponding gains, you should realize you have deficient comprehensive calibers to lead troops. If you don't realize this and just behave yourself as usual, you will just entangle yourself deeper and deeper, and no one can help you.

　　帅将能力之差异直接呈现于其兵种能力的高下，唇齿关连。对"大事勿用或密事勿用"者需酌情调配，对"凡事勿用"者则需三思了！感情用事与意气用事同样坏事与窝囊！

　　Quality of the troops reflects caliber of a marshal or general, and vice versa. A marshal or general that can not fulfill significant or confidential actions should be appropriately assigned, and a marshal or general that can not fulfill any events should deserve thorough consideration. Handling affairs with emotions is as harmful and annoying as that without intelligence.

弱兵充斥就是冗员屯积！兵之强弱取决于后天的培育、帅将的督导、修正与心态结盟，乃帅将领军水平之写照，骗不了人。难道你宁可奉行精兵制或扛着沉重包袱走下去？

Too many weak troops just indicating overstaffing. Quality of soldiers is dependent on cultivation, supervision and correction by the marshal or general, and just portrays caliber of the marshal or general. Do you prefer to lead powerful troops or proceed with a big headache?

"恶意的口诛笔伐、违心的夸赞、沉默的姑息"，乃领军者的三大害，逐渐引领兵员战败沙场、体无完肤！善意的批评让人难受但未必是坏事！

Oral and written condemnation out of malicious purposes, false compliment and acquiescent appeasement are three don't for commanders. Commanders of this kind will lead their troops to failure and loss step by step. Criticism out of goodwill may be embarrassing, but not necessarily bad.

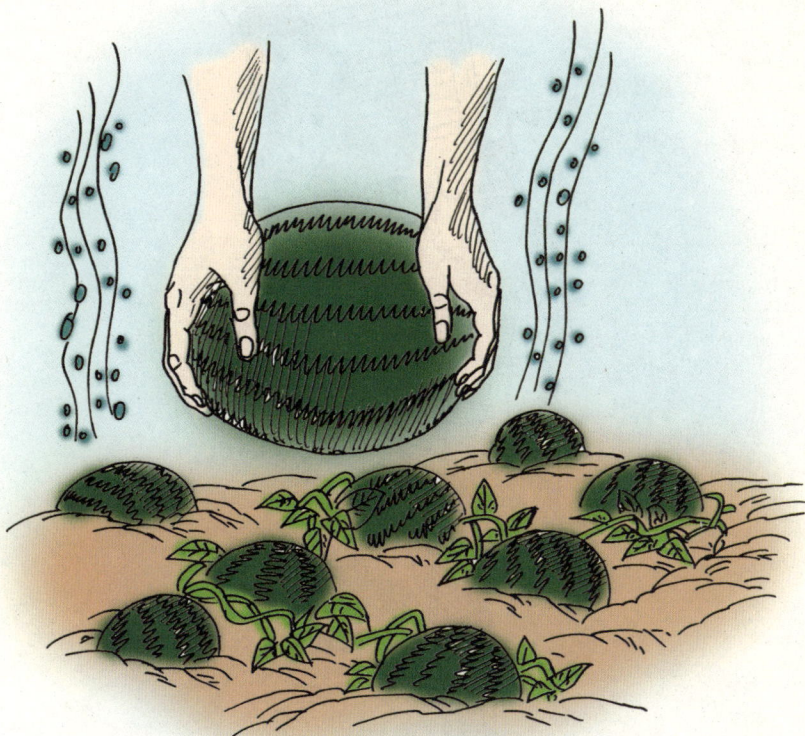

为帅、将者必须勇于承担责任, 但又需相互分担成果及压力! 单方面的受压或掩藏难处乃不成熟表现, 徒令战果或进度受损, 贻误整体, 那样不叫伟大, 实属肤浅!

A marshal or general must be prepared to face the music, and share the fruit and pressure with his men. Any unilateral burden of responsibility or cover of hardships just evidences immaturity, hampers the result or progress, and does harm to the overall situation. This is not great, but skin-deep.

　　真正尽忠、尽责的将领多持"领导无处不在、任务时刻达标"的心态处事，无须刻意做秀或逢迎：精明干练的领导以绩效作证！

　　A really loyal and responsible general typically takes the attitude that leadership exists anywhere and tasks are fulfilled anytime, and does not have to show up or flatter. A wise and capable leader proves himself with performance.

　　帅将间的互助互信源于性格、手法及绩效的结合！不达标及冥顽无改进者自然丧失讨价还价地位，纵有舌粲莲花或免死金牌也不管用。成败得失自有公论！

　　Mutual trust between a marshal and his general originates from combination of nature, skills and performance. If a marshal or general is not eligible, and stubbornly reluctant to improve, he will certainly lose the leeway to bargain, even if he has a forked tongue or powerful background. Public opinions will definitely conclude his success or failure and gains or loss.

一个马虎、草率、失职的将领，很难带出尽忠尽责又善战的兵。此等"混将"誓被上下唾弃、咎由自取！越抗拒绩效考核则越显其心虚无能。怎样的处事手法衍生怎样的下属，骗了自己骗不了人！

It is hard for a careless, reckless and incompetent general to train loyal, responsible and strong soldiers. Such a despicable general will be abandoned by the inferior and superior, and should have only himself to blame. The harder he resists performance check, the less confident he is in his ability. A general just produces the men of his own kind.

　　强悍专横的帅、器重务实的将，以战绩挂帅；优柔寡断的帅、依托表面功夫的将，以放任为先。两者孰优孰劣，时移势易，见仁见智。

A valiant and bossy marshal favors practical generals, and prioritizes military successes. An indecisive marshal relies on generals who talk big, and prioritizes appeasement. Time is the best judge to determine which is superior or inferior.

　　一样粮草养百样兵！兵员素质、水平的优劣师承其将帅的手法。小样的头出小样的人，大度的将出大度的兵。

The same army provisions feed greatly different soldiers. Quality and level of soldiers depend on means of their marshal and general. A narrow-minded marshal or general generate equally narrow-minded soldiers, and a broad-minded marshal or general cultivate equally broad-minded soldiers.

一朝天子未必一朝臣！视乎君臣将帅间的磨合、水平、实践与统一步伐，此乃定律！你欲作基石或包袱？

A new emperor does not always clear out the senior officials of his predecessor. This depends on cooperation, level, practice and uniform step between the emperor and officials, and the marshal and general. This is a definite rule. Do you want to be a cornerstone or burden?

天降甘霖，泽披物流先驱者；
恩逢雨露，福惠货代有心人！

God Bestows a Timely Rain,
and Benefits Logistics Vanguards;
God Bestows a Favour,
and Benefits Prepared Freight Forwarders.

球喻篇

The Chapter on "World Cup Match"

球队致胜：团结是基础，定位清晰、扬长避短、找切入点一蹴即破是关键！专业的门将可力保不失。那么，让怕球者当门将结果又如何？

Unity is the base for a team's success, and the clear orientation, the strengthening of strong points and the overwhelming of weak points, as well as the cut in the point of penetration to accomplish its goal in one step are the key! A professional goalkeeper is able to directly prevent the opposite team from scoring by defending the goal! What the results will be, if a goalkeeper afraid of ball is designated to act as the goalkeeper?

　　明星队"皇马"所向披靡，全仗各路精英汇聚、配以外包装、良好的战术运用、现场发挥默契及团队效应而成就伟业！试把其拆散或错配，看"结果"如何？

　　The star team "Real Madrid" is invincible, depending on the gathering of elites, the excellent use of tactics, perfect on-the-spot performance and strong teamwork spirit! How it will be, if the team breaks up or wrongly mixes its players?

自称多优秀、专业、忠诚的前锋，如不积极、主动冲锋，突破后防，寻隙扣门，则言过于实！有见过散漫的前锋可破网的？

If a striker doesn't strike, pierce through defence or seek opportunities to shoot actively, he is just overstating himself, no matter how excellent, profession and loyal he claims to be. Have you seen any rambling striker succeed in defending the goal?

球赛结束前五分钟反败为胜的例子多的是！究其原因：对方自以为是、轻敌！己方坚持奋战、主动进取、顽强信念所致！这与运气扯不上关系。

There are many examples that a team turns defeat into victory within the five minutes before the game ends! It may be owing to its competitor's underestimation or self-righteous or its persevering struggle, active aggression or firm belief! It has nothing to do with fortune!

　　球星"贝克汉姆"有迷人的外包装，加上精湛球技才实至名归。试想没团队的后勤或总体配合又如何？

　　Soccer star Beckham is famous for his charming appearance and consummate techniques. How he will be if there is no perfect cooperation among all players or the team's excellent logistics service?

无严格的教练无优秀的球队；无公平的球规无公平的赛果，企管亦然！

No strict coach, no excellent team! No fair-minded referee, no fair results! Enterprise management is just like this!

球员连场激战肯定疲态毕露。要确保发挥最佳状态、夺取战果，必须注意保健、营养、放松。休养就能生息、生利！

After consecutive games, players must be tired! They shall take care of their health, nutrition and relaxation to maintain good moods and win more games. Relaxation brings vigor and interest!

绿茵场上的共同目标只有一个：必胜！试想如没有黄、红牌制度，球场誓演变为战场！至于球员被调出肯定有原因：或不规范、或不在状态、或与队员不一致……归根究底：乃确保团队的"必胜"目标不受损害！

The common goal on the green meadow-surfaced court is success! The court will certainly become a battlefield just assuming that there is no red card to foul players or yellow card to warn them! There must be some reasons if the referee sends any player off, such as his non-compliance with rules, his bad moods or disharmony with his team. And the fundamental purpose is to assure a success!

　　严谨认真的教练于赛前必先了解球员的体质、心态以及装备才派员上阵。能自我发掘问题的球员不多，这才显得积极、专业、时刻督导、尽责的教练的重要性！

　　A precise and serious-minded coach shall not ask football players to take part in contest before they check their constitution, mind and outfit, because only a few of players can notice their own problems. This reflects the importance of an active, professional, diligent and pious coach!

英格兰与葡萄牙本势均力敌，但英格兰以缺一员之劣势亦可斗至点球，全仗精兵制结合、无穷斗志与坚决不懈的信念使然！是团队雄心的表现，与运气无关。败亦无愧！

The teams of England and Portugal match each other in strength. Although the England team is reduced to a 10 man team, all players still keep their combative and persevering faith and contend till they win penalties finally. It is a reflection of their ambition and has nothing to do with the fortune! They will regret nothing even if they lose the game!

意大利排众而出，成功夺魁，绝非意外：看每场赛事，各参赛者全情投入、团结不抢功、专业技术得以发挥、战术运用得宜、充足的体能…全可引以为鉴！是帅将兵的完美结合而促成战果！

The Italian football team wins the World Cup, not by accident! In every contest, every participant is fully engaged and united. They don't rush to rob awards for themselves, bring their professional technologies into full play, use tactics properly and maintain ample physical energy in the whole contest. They set good examples for other teams! It is perfect cooperation between every participant that makes them succeed finally!

　　球员被逐出场，输的不单是球赛，而是名声！再一次印证"处变不惊、遇事沉着面对"之真理！

　　A football player loses not only the game but his reputation if he is hoofed out of the court! It once again proves the truth that one shall stay calm in the face of upheaval and be imperturbable in the face of matters!

天降甘霖，泽披物流先驱者；
恩逢雨露，福惠货代有心人！
God Bestows a Timely Rain,
and Benefits Logistics Vanguards;
God Bestows a Favour,
and Benefits Prepared Freight Forwarders.

心术篇

The Chapter on "Frame of mind"

不因眼前货量攀升而乱了套；不因经营项目激增或版图扩大而添压力，遇强越强。在淡季中做到开源节流、逆流而上，将勤补拙不会见效，"以智补勤"才有胜望！

Don't get into panic on rising sales, don't feel excessive pressure from surging business scope or territory, and just get stronger in face of tougher situations. Broaden the sources of income and reduce expenditures in the low season, and forge ahead in face of adversity. To make up clumsiness with diligence does not make difference, and only to reinforce intelligence with diligence is likely to succeed.

　　天霖企管艺术文化精要内含环环相扣、贯彻到底的处事精神：是科学管治，提高效率而不是划分界线，助长官僚歪风！同样，内部会议乃共同"参政、议政"为把事做到最好，并不是予管理者搭建演戏或较劲场地。不懂开会精粹者绝对不是好的管理者！

　　The essence of FORWARD management culture embodies the spirit of close collaboration between each link and clear distribution of responsibility to each person. This is scientific governance for the purpose of improving efficiency, not drawing a clear line between different links or promoting bureaucracy. Similarly, internal meetings are the place for the staff to participate in and discuss corporate affairs, not the occasion for managers to show up or the arena to battle others. A manager who does not understand the essence of meetings is never a good manager.

　　有责任心者，对人对事对己均负责，哪怕水平、学识比不上他人，亦终有出头之日！细看没出息者多为没责任心者，幸运之神不轻易眷顾，纵有瞬间的光芒亦难以持久绽放！

　　A manager with consciousness of responsibility is responsible for others, business and himself, and eventually become outstanding, even if he is inferior to others in capacity and knowledge. In contrast, unpromising people are usually those without consciousness of responsibility, and are not easily favored by the Lady Luck. Even if they make some successes once, they will have much difficulty in keeping such success lasting.

一个尽责尽职尽心的人肯定累，但只要懂得自我调整顽劣错误手法，自然活得丰盛有意义！相对那些马虎草率推搪又冥顽不灵者，一定活得艰苦，纵表面风光，实内心交战！

A responsible, devoted and enthusiastic person must feel tired. However, he will lead a meaningful life as long as he knows to correct his wrong methods. In contrary, an irresponsible, careless and stubborn person must live a hard life and fatigue his heart, even though he seems to have dignity.

　　真正忠诚的主管行事皆以"心"为公司出发，不论直接或间接、对本部或他部，皆和衷共济地不断开源节流，那些卖口乖或乘势邀功者乃伪忠诚，只管个人得失、不理公司总体步伐，将难以立足于天霖！

　　A truly responsible and loyal manager does everything for the sake of the company out of his heart, directly or indirectly, for his own division or brother divisions, and works together with his teammates to continuously broaden the sources of income and reduce expenditures. A manager that talks big and takes credit for others' achievements is not really loyal, just thinks of his personal interests, and he will be hard to stay in FORWARD.

　　天霖主管必须学"吃的文化"：做市场大小通吃，不因小客户而怠慢；对竞争搞事者吃得定；在内部管理团队内吃得开；最重要是能吃苦、干活不怕吃亏！

　　FORWARD's managers must learn the "culture to eat", namely, never neglect any customer in marketing whether a big customer or a small customer; cope with competitors; gain support from the internal management team; and the most important is to endure and work hard without considering personal gains.

有容乃大

　　天霖人一般都能干、聪明、有情有义，我为你们喝彩；但公务上往往过于钻研无关痛痒的小节而浪费时间，或有意无意设计人为矛盾，未免不够大气！新时代已然开始，人站高点、看远点、心宽点才能突破！别对自己较劲。

　　FORWARD staff are mostly capable, clever and considerate, and I applaud for you. However, excess attention to trivial is merely waste of time and to create contradictions on purpose is a little narrow-minded. A new era has started, and we should stand higher, see farther, and get more broad-minded to make new breakthroughs. Don't entangle yourself.

　　知错真改比屡错屡犯好；以眼代耳比以耳代目强；将智补勤比将勤补拙胜！一个放松自己的主管肯定放纵下属；推卸逃避的肯定受下属鄙视；闭门造秀而不知下属工作表现的，肯定令全仁受制约、自己也飞不起来！

　　It is better to realize and correct mistakes than repeat them, it is better to replace your ears with eyes than vice versa, and it is better to make up diligence with intelligence than supplement clumsiness with diligence. A self-indulging manager is certain to spoil his men, a manager staving off responsibilities is definite to be despised by his men, and a manager turning a blind eye to performance of his men is set to restrain his colleagues and not to take off either.

　　团队作战取决于默契，默契源于沟通与信任：这有赖自身待人接物及一贯的处事手法使然！忌孤高自赏、杯弓虫影、闭门造戏！管理者以反映"事实"寻根究底、对症下药为己任：可取！讲"事非"与听"是非"肯定破坏团队和谐：可悲！

　　A team depends on privity to win battles, and privity originates from communications and trust. Trust forms on your constant manner to behave yourself. You should not indulge in self-admiration, get caught in skepticism or turn a blind eye on facts. A manager deserves praise if he discovers the ultimate cause for problems through facts, and takes corresponding countermeasures. A manager is poor if he tells the fact untruly, hears the fact wrongly, and spoils the harmony of the whole team.

　　惯性拖延工作乃耽误商机、祸延整体的写照；一直的被动、滞后是不思突破、引火自焚的根由；经常欠沟通多因缺乏自信心或心虚作祟，与能力无关！

　　Habitual delay in work just costs business opportunities and undermines the overall situation. Constant absence of initiatives and lag are just the root for reluctance to make progress and look for trouble. Frequent shortage of communications usually stems from insufficient confidence, and does not relate to capacity.

　　个人水平、教养与其工作及社会成就不一定成正比！可从日常表现直接体现其形象优劣、影响深远。趁未被"定型"前扭转是上策，执迷不悔则孤身上路，越走越远！

　　Personal ability and education are not necessarily in proportion to his work and social achievements, and his daily behavior can directly mirror his image and have profound influences. It is advisable to change his way before he finalizes his behavior, and stupid to go farther and farther on the wrong way.

　　鹬蚌相争，敌人得利；掩耳盗铃、甜言蜜语骗自己，与自杀无疑。醉过方知酒浓、疼过方懂刑重；既无法突破自己就先让自己疼吧！物先腐而后生、人感疼才自觉成长。

　　Any internal conflict benefits only the enemy, and deceiving himself with sweet words is just tantamount to suicide. Only after getting drunk, will you know how strong alcohol is, and only after pains, will you understand rigidity of penalties. Now that you cannot defeat yourself, just ache. Materials will gain fresh vitality only after deterioration, and a person will grow up only after pains.

　　天霖宗旨乃务实发展、用人唯材！当你感觉心寒时，先照镜子、自我查找丑态！也许是心虚作祟啊。

FORWARD aims to pursue growth with practicality and use people by capacity. When you feel depressed, first look at yourself in the mirror to find your shortcomings. This is possibly because of your guilty conscience.

有压力未必即时见进步，受责难未必是坏事！只怕错而不改或不分对错而已！需知道报忧比报喜更重要，可先知先觉分析病源、对症下药！过多的粉饰升平乃自我催眠，不思进取！

Pressure is not necessarily bound for advancement and arraignment is not necessarily a bad thing! We are afraid only of cling to the mistake instead of correcting it or making no distinction between right and wrong! We should understand that reporting the bad is more important than reporting the good. This can provide us a foresight to analyze the source of mistakes and work out corresponding solutions! Excessive whitewash is self-cheating and self-gratification.

　　对事不对人、律己律人、常以公司发展为己任者肯定赢多输少；搞分化绝不会有好日子过。武断不叫果断；主观不是主见！

Those concerning themselves with facts and not with individuals, blaming themselves as they would blame others and regarding the company's development as their own responsibilities will surely gain more and lose less; and those carrying out disunity and polarization will certainly have a hard time. Arbitrary is not decisive and subjective is not definite!

　　你试立足高处看同一的人、物、事，感觉可会一样？相反，你情愿一辈子被人仰望或平视？不同的心态引发不同的价值观而衍生不同的处事手法。事实胜于诡辩，业绩证明一切，企业与团队共谋发展乃核心。

　　Do you the same if you try to judge the same person or the same thing from a higher position? Otherwise, will you be content to stay at a higher or the same level with others in your whole life? Different minds result in different views of value and different ways for treating problems. Facts speak louder than words, and performance prove all. The core is that the company and its team shall strive for development together.

　　坚持、毅力是成功的踏脚石；但过分的、自以为是的硬坚持、瞎毅力就是绊脚石，害己害人，早晚闯祸！"改变"不免流于短暂、片面，或于受压下才驱使自己无奈的变；"蜕变"乃痛定思痛，狠下心肠，强逼自己突破、革新之变，有长久效益！

Persistence and perseverance are stepping-stones for success! While overstrong self-righteous persistence or blind-minded perseverance are stumbling blocks and are to injure others and self and bring about troubles sooner or later! A "change" is always temporary and unilateral and often results from pressure; a "complete change" is to make up mind to break through or innovate after the recall from painful experiences and has long-term benefits!

　　"忘记"与"拖延"是隐性的"不负责任"，视乎经理人对个别任务的重视程度来判别其水平、能力及处事手法的真伪！

　　"Forget" or "delay" are recessive "irresponsibility". The two lie on managers' attention to every task and distinguish whether their capacity and ways for treating problems are genuine or fake!

　　宁各尽本分，团结互助齐达标；毋自我催眠，孤芳自赏骗自己。小事不会做，大事成不了；大事跟不上，小节实糊涂！不要求舌粲莲花、滔滔伟论，只求结果齐达标！

　　To meet the target, everyone had better fulfill their duties and unit each other rather than solely indulge in self-righteousness or self-admiration. They shall begin with trifles or they can't accomplish important tasks; if they can't catch up with others in important tasks, they may be confused by some details. There is no need to talk glibly or spout eloquent speeches, and the only need is to meet targets!

在山脚下跑得快、站得稳，不代表具备即时登高条件；试先立台阶上比较差别：看极目多远、心胸多宽、能力多寡，才决定爬多高吧！天系山峰不易闯，迎头痛改未算迟！

The ability to run fast and stand steadily at the foot of the mountain doesn't represent the capacity to climb high. Try to stand on the stair to compare with others. How high can you climb depends on how far can you reach, how wide your breadth of mind can be and how many capacities you have had! You should not rush to the hard corner and it's never too late for you to turn around from the hard corner!

　　当你认定上级专横，并处处针对时，也许真这样子，也许事出有因。应冷静思己的对与错才定论：可有尽己本分或执迷不改？闲时常思己过，动时多取战果。

　　When you feel your manager is bossy and always hostile with you, this is maybe the case, or something must have happened. Calm down and think over whether you have fulfilled your duties or have struck to your mistakes before coming to a conclusion. Think more about yourself when free and you will gain more when taking actions.

　　公司正值蜕变期，难免衍生新事物、新工作。不怕难，用积极、进取心全力以赴就一定成功！当你把事业作为工作时，多少存侥幸、敷衍心态；但当你把工作视为事业时，自会逐渐融入大和谐圈内，你将发现人生多姿彩、工作满丰盈！

　　A company's change is always accompanied by the emergence of new things and new opportunities. Please do not be afraid. Make efforts actively. You will make it! You may have flukey and perfunctory minds, when regarding the career as your work, and you may gradually be in harmony and found your life colorful when regarding the work as your career!

　　智者应时刻让人陪同照镜子，待别人对镜中的你认定为完美才是真完美！孤芳自赏有何难哉？秦桧与潘仁美互嘲的例子比比皆是。

A wise man shall ask his accompanist to look at him from the mirror. He can't be really perfect unless his accompanist thinks so! How hard for a man to indulge in self-admiration? Examples can be found everywhere, like Qin Hui and Pan Renmei.

　　当你感觉天天忙晕时，也许是公司或本部处于急速发展中，又或者下属不力，影响整体效率！这总比天天无所事事、被动敷衍、自以为工作及管治已然到顶、不需对上下负责好！试学写工作日志自我检查工作量，反映真伪。

　　When you feel busy all day long, it is either because the company or your division grows fast, or because your men are incompetent and affect the overall efficiency. However, it is better than idle about, walk through or believe the management has been too strict to take charge of the subordinates! Learn to write diary to check your workload.

　　对劣质行为姑息，就是纵容，结果乃"种瓜得瓜"不难想象！"姑息"肯定源于自身的不正。试想企管者如漠视公司规章制度，企能管好本部或发挥麾下功能？忠于工作、制度才称得上忠诚、负责；除非上级亦姑息处事，歪风渐成！

　　To be indulgent towards improper behaviors is to lead to bad results! Indulgence certainly results from managers' improper behaviors. Can a manager take good charge of its division or make full use of his subordinates, if he brushes aside the articles of associates? A manager is not really loyal or responsible unless he is committed to work and regulations. Contagion will not be rife unless managers indulge improper behaviors.

　　"自律"乃自我遵行纪律、自掌尺度；"尽责"指尽忠职守，责任到己到人。健全的企管流程、政策皆依托此才得以健康发展，违者无疑"自尽"于天霖。

　　"Self-discipline" is the trait of practicing self discipline and exercising sound judgment. "Responsibility" is to be committed to duties and assign duties to individuals. Upon this, a perfect enterprise management process and policy can develop healthily and any disobedience will undoubtedly destroy FORWARD.

　　绩效考核成败取决于管理者水平及众人的认知与投入！要推行无阻必先除毒瘤、去顽劣自恃者！"中央程式监控管理委员会"既属民主墙，又是钟馗爷，无惧千夫所指。适当的牺牲在所难免，扭曲的裙带关系需同步抚平！

　　The success of the performance appraisal system hinges on managers' capacity and every employee's recognition and devotion! The disturbed and the self-relied shall be cleared up before the implementation of such. The Central Process Monitoring & Management Committee serves both the platform for democratic management and the magic weapon to fight non-conforming activities and people, and fears no criticism. Appropriate sacrifice is unavoidable and the twisty nepotism shall be neatened simultaneously!

　　"诚信"乃待人处事之本;"伶俐"绝不是伶牙俐齿,砌词掩饰罪状,甚至以权谋私,欺上瞒下! 小聪明者可稍躲一时,无本事者则累积错处、贪得无厌,迟早不攻自破,引火烧身! 天霖一脉自有天道护航。

　　"Sincerity"is the base for getting along with people and dealing with matters. "Clever"is absolutely not glibness, concealment of mistakes, usurping of administrative power for private interests or deceiving of superiors and deluding of subordinates! A man playing petty trick can only dodge for a period of time. The incompetent always accumulate faults. And the avaricious will collapse sooner or later! FORWARD's development will subject to the natural law.

　　人贵自知、人戒自恃、人应自律：遵此三大原则，肯定与时并进，傲立天地之间！成功之道贵乎诚、正、勤、律：皆属心态使然！掩饰、逃躲，乃自断前程，自灭于社群的通病！

　　A person is wise to know his limitations, keep away from self-reliance, and remain in self-discipline. He can advance steadily and stand proudly if obeying these principles! The success depends on sincerity, righteousness, diligence and self-image, which all arise from attitudes! Any dodge or escape is to damage your career and yourself in the social group.

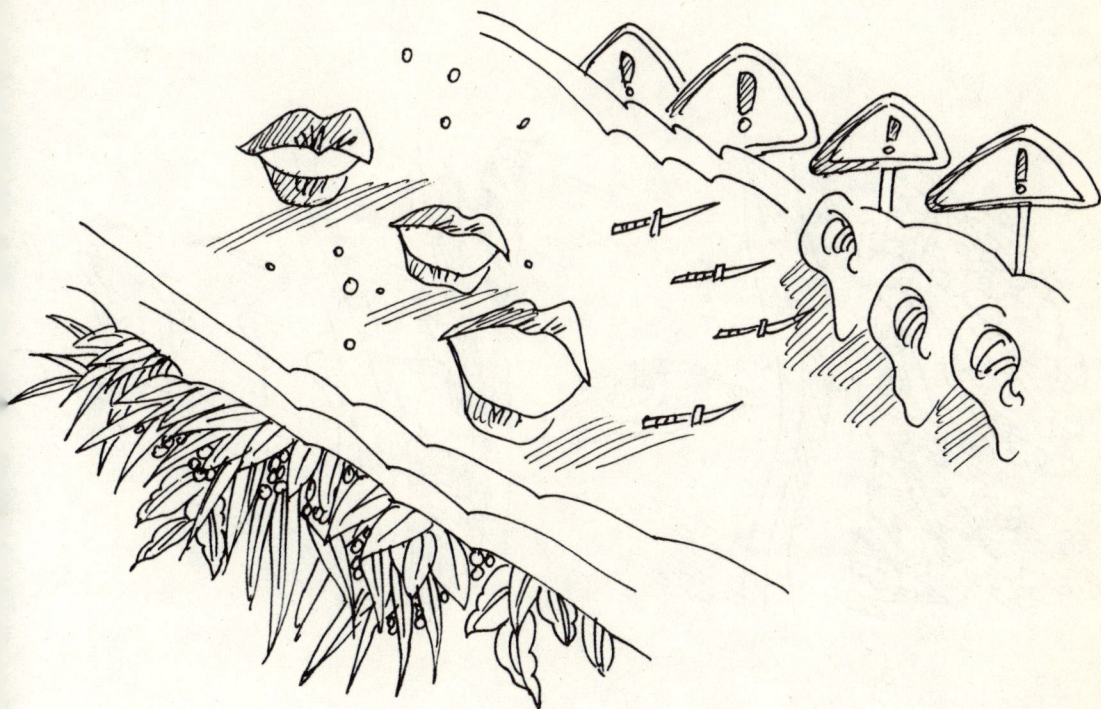

漂亮的谎言与现实同样残酷！别人对你的歌颂或恭维未必是实话,勿沾沾自喜；个人魅力不一定体现于外观或学识的高下；能忠于公司、团队,而又认真面对工作的,自然绩效有功,魅力自成！旁人的眼睛比嘴巴实际。

Sweet lies are just as cruel as the reality. Don't take great pride when hailed or flattered by others, because such undue compliment or flattery is not necessarily heart-felt words. Personal charm does not necessarily take the form of a good look or profound knowledge. In fact, a person will naturally achieve a lot and earn his charm with loyalty to the company and his team as well as devotion to work. What others see speaks louder than what they say.

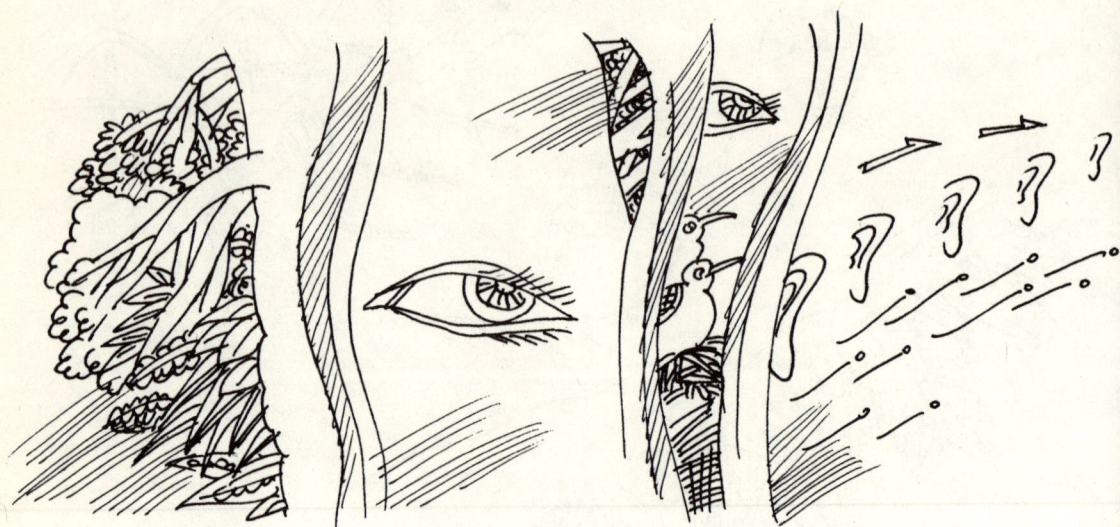

要成功先学心胸、想长久先尽责任！包容心不等同包庇或纵容；是酌情宽恕、不结怨、不记恨！心宽自然路宽、心广、资源足。听违心的赞美肯定比听实在的忠告、批评来得舒泰？见仁见智。

Breast comes before success, and responsibility comes before permanence. Forgiveness is no synonym to defense or connivance, but case-specific mercy and to let bygones be bygones. A broad mind is naturally rewarded with enriched channels, a care-free mood and abundant resources. Does false compliment surely bring comfort than true advice and criticism? This depends.

　　当一个问题反映到你处，你随即有十个、甚至更多的理由、理论、理解、理性反馈时，这不叫解决问题，只是砌词推诿，弥补过失、顽劣不改；你不累，旁人也累！与其自我催眠编战果，不如实事求是显进步！惯性逃避与绕圈子答问同样拙劣。客户有耐性陪你绕吗？

　　In face of a problem, even if you have ten and even more reasons, theories, understandings and rationality to feed back, you are not solving the problem, but avoiding it, making up for the mistake and sticking to the bad habit. Even if you don't feel tired, others will. It is better to take substantial actions for improvement than deceiving yourself with false performance. It is as clumsy and inferior to avoid habitually as to beat about the bush. Do customers have enough patience to play with you?

当你自觉工作过量时，多半是获赏识、能者多劳又下属缺助力；总比无所事事、自认无用武之地又赋闲不自求进取好得多：事在人为！

When you feel extra work, this is mostly because you have been appreciated by your boss. You have to work more while your men are unable to help you well. However, this is anyway much better than to idle about, think of yourself highly while having no chance, and refuse to progress. It all depends on human efforts.

　　管理人丢了自身的责、权、利、诚信及威望多源于：散漫、偷懒、自我忽悠，活该！至于工作滞后，轻重失据，多因自我中心作怪：或逃避、或存侥幸心，怪不了人！肯学、肯干、肯海纳智者意见者，才显自身的超然！

　　A manager loses his responsibility, right, gain, reputation and prestige, mostly the result of self-relaxation, laziness and self-deceit, and just serves himself right. Delay in work and confused order of priority usually come as the consequence of self-centeredness, either to avoid or harbor false luck, and this should not blame others. Keen to learn, work and take advice from the intelligent, a manager will display his broadmindedness.

　　怕背责任者越要背更大的负面责任；越想逃避问题的，则越往后退、越陷越深；坚持己见属有原则的表现：可取！但不分就里，过于坚持的则肯定进步不了，迟早碰壁：可惜！天道酬勤，勇谋兼备无俱向前闯！

　　If a person is reluctant to take responsibility, he will just keep himself far away from serious negative responsibility. If a person wishes to avoid problems, he will just step back and go farther in the wrong direction. Sticking to one's own opinions represents adhesion to principles, which deserves praise. However, blind-minded adhesion will lead no progress, and be rebuffed sooner or later. Pity it! God favors the diligent, and just forge ahead with both courage and intelligence.

　　何谓可耻？白拿钱不干活的、想自己不想团队的、为自身利益不为公司的、巧言掩饰不切实际的、厚颜推诿又吃里扒外的！可耻与无耻匹配，诸色人种得而诛之、弃之。

　　What is shame? Get paid without work, consider himself only instead of the team, care about the interest of himself only rather than the company, talk with a forked tongue without considering the reality, stave off responsibility and betray the company! Shame and cheekiness accompany, and everybody can blame a person of this kind.

　　内部矛盾源于对与错的执著，矛盾加剧拘泥于相互的沟通手法及心态纠缠。孤掌不一定难鸣，看凝聚力深浅而定；可孤芳自赏肯定自我封闭，如井底蛙般自我封锁、自我摧毁！越高层就越要显和谐。

　　Internal contradiction originates from conflict between the right and the wrong, and strengthening contradiction stems from mutual communications and controversial psychological status. A single palm can also play the game, which depends on the cohesive force. Self-administration will definitely result in self-enclosure, very limited outlook and self-destruction. The higher position you take, the more important harmony will be.

民企无"铁饭碗"。越规范的民企越为能者打造璀璨的仕途！铁哥们儿更应拿出铁一般的干劲来展示实力，否则与豆腐渣无异，帮倒忙！然雌雄肯定有别，工作上则男女平等，相辅相成才有胜算。只怕是男生女格、女使男气，有失和睦团结之风。

A private enterprise offers no secure job. The more regular a private enterprise is, the brighter prospect it will create for the capable. Men should fledge his muscles to display your strength, and otherwise you are just a white elephant. Men and women differ, but are equal in work. They will only succeed by supplementing each other. The only concern is that womanish men and mannish women will spoil harmony and teamwork.

上级对你严词厉色，一丝不苟，肯定难受，此乃"苦口良药"；对你百般迁就，置之不管，省事，此乃"糖衣毒药"，各有所好！看你心病多重而已！

Your boss's severity and strictness with you must make you unhappy, but can cure your disease although bitter. However, if your boss indulges you and leaves you alone, this will ruin you though sweet. Everybody has his own preference, and this depends on how serious your emotional disease is.

　　承诺就是诚信！当你向上级或同僚多次有意无意破坏工作诚诺时，个人形象亦难以维持！工作就是工作！切勿有所恃：恃资历、关系或能力。天霖不吃这套！上下级捆绑一起共甘苦！

Commitment comes as credit. When you break your working commitment intentionally or unintentionally, you will just spoil your personal image. Work is work! Don't depend on anything, record of service, relationship or capacity. FORWARD does not buy this story. The superior and inferior should share sweetness and bitterness.

客观处事者皆由两面看；主观自恃者多是头脑发热、模糊不清、礼教不明。现实社会只重结果、不重过程，没对错之分，试稍作心态转移，将发现彩霞片片，人生满姿采！劳而得获比不劳而获实际得多。公道自在人心！

An objective person looks at both sides of a coin, while a subjective person does not calm down, have clear distinction or know the ethics well. The realistic society only stresses the result and neglects the process, and this is no problem which is right or wrong. Just try to change your position, and you will brush away your bad emotions and find a colorful life. To gain with pains is much more practical than gains without pains. Justice naturally lies in the public.

天降甘霖，泽披物流先驱者；
恩逢雨露，福惠货代有心人！
God Bestows a Timely Rain,
and Benefits Logistics Vanguards;
God Bestows a Favour,
and Benefits Prepared Freight Forwarders.

商战篇

The Chapter on "Commercial War"

　　天霖致力开拓的"神州物流网络"是大伙儿的事，是天霖人的事！要认真、坚持，切勿蜻蜓点水，集体做坏秀！少怨气、多改进；消错误、增智慧！

　　The "FORWARD Logistics Alliance" which FORWARD is striving to build is a business for everyone here. Everybody shall be earnest and persistent and shall go into matters deeply, not just scratch the surface! Just complain less and improve more. Try to eliminate mistakes and increase wisdom!

　　你已重新投入许胜不许败的战阵了，首天上班先召开本部工作例会温故知新，再统筹跨部门会议为"狗年大腾飞"作深入交流！既属拜年又可即时启动工作步伐、抢占先机，一举两得！

　　You have just come back to a war that you can only win and never lose. On the first day of your work, you will attend a regular meeting of your division to review previous works and then a trans-division meeting to conduct in-depth discussion about"a big jump in the year of dog"! This goes like a New Year's visit and the beginning of work in the new year. It takes the initiate and serves a double purpose!

又是双喜临门的一天！随着多个网点的扩充,再体现天霖锐不可挡的发展势头。天霖人都是许胜不许败的领头人！不因新增项目多而自乱阵脚,反而是发挥领兵、献策、歼敌的好证明！

A double blessing descends upon FORWARD again! The expansion of its existing outlets mirrors its development with irresistible force and that all of its staff are leaders that can only win and never lose! It is also a good reflection of its excellent ability in leadership, intelligence and performance and its calmness in the midst of fast business expansion.

商战存起伏，人生有起落；只要坚定信念，群策群力，放开怀抱面对美好将来，则事业与人生俱丰盛，两全其美！

Just like the life, commercial competition is full of ups and downs. You will enjoy a successful career as well as a perfect life, as long as you corroborate your belief, pool the wisdom and efforts of everyone and open your mind to get ready to welcome a bright future!

　　构筑坚实的礼貌服务城墙绝非朝夕之事，推倒它只弹指之间！是"你"的问题，责无旁贷！天霖人是干细活、不干"粗"活的！被投诉者及其上级"好自为之"了！接受事实，勇于改进吧！

　　The attitude of sincere politeness can't be formed within a short period of time, but can be destroyed in a short moment. If it is attributed to your own faults, there is no shirking of your responsibility! FORWARD peers are careful, but not careless! The appellee and its manager shall go ahead! Accept the facts and try to improve!

　　企业不因规模大小自居，是因其内部管理体系的严谨、管理层执行力的认真及管理团队手法的成熟来界定高低：礼貌服务不可松、风险管理不放手、综合促销不退让！

　　A company is superior, because of its strict internal management system, the earnest execution by its management and the mature management methods, but not because of its scale. Polite service can't be eased, risk management can't be neglected and comprehensive promotion can't be compromised!

天霖企管乃艺术哲学！对事不对人＝凝聚团队力量；礼貌服务够完善＝加速综合销售抢滩强；风险操作零瑕疵＝专心拓展新领域；环环相扣沟通紧＝有形无形。管理意识无处不在！

The FORWARD's management is actually a philosophy of art! The attitude of concerning things with facts and not with individuals can agglomerate the power of its team. Polite and all-around services can quicken comprehensive sales and fast expansion! Zero-defect operation can guarantee its single-minded exploration of new fields. Close linkage and instant communication are tangible and intangible. FORWARD's management thoughts are everywhere!

　　商战胜败取决于管理者心态与手法，"三心两意"是关键：决心、信心、团结心＋诚意、战意＝同步取胜；私心、被动逃避心、内斗心＋漫不经意、自鸣得意＝淘汰出局！

　　The key to the success in commercial competition is managers' minds and methods. Determination, confidence and comity, together with sincerity and the willingness to fight, will lead to a success. Selfishness, passive escape, and internal power struggle, together with insouciance and self-satisfaction, will lead to a failure!

时移世易，现今乃打信息战、团体战的年代；单挑肯定输得快、跌得惨！天霖体系内无个人主义存在！只重"结果"！

The world has come into a new era! Nowadays, it is an era of information competition and team match. Anyone who wants to fight on his own efforts will end with a crucial failure quickly! FORWARD's management system has no individualism and its only focus is on result!

　　市场促销取胜之道乃重点突出自身的优势、特色，策略性的扬长避短来突显及抬高自己的"卖点"，以激发对方的购买欲，好比应聘面试一样。传统的降价用于成熟的市场里难以破冰，必须有"招"才行！

　　The key to the success in marketing promotion is to inspire customers' desire to purchase by giving prominence to your own advantages and highlighting your "selling points" through developing your advantages while avoiding your shortcomings. It is just like an interview. The traditional method of price-cutting doesn't function well in mature market and talents recruitment is the only way out!

　　瞬间的闪烁不一定永恒，短暂的挫败未必就灭绝，这乃成熟市场的定律。高峰处须不断寻隙求变保有新鲜感；低迷时思己过，充分发挥现有资源，找切入点突破市场障碍，则成功在望！

　　An instant flash is not necessarily permanent, and any temporary set-back is not necessarily failed completely! This is the law for a mature market. The success will be within your grasp, if you seek chance to change when reaching the top position and take full advantage of existing resources to seek the points of penetration to break barriers when pondering over your own mistakes in a downturn.

人生充满机遇与挑战！没有解决不了的事，更没有开拓不了的市场！视乎理性的坚持、技巧的定位、周详的市场分析及和谐积极的团队心。要业绩超标，易如反掌！

The life is full of opportunities and challenges. There is no matter that can't be solved, let alone any market that can't be explored! It depends on reasonable perseverance, skilled orientation, detailed market analysis and harmonious and active teamwork spirit. If so, the performance will go beyond expectation as easy as turning one's hand over.

　　服务行业的成功在于全体上下皆以"服务"为主！其真谛乃以"服从"与"务实"态度待客。越有难度，越帮得上，则越见天霖的突出；不断的为自己、为同僚开脱徒令客户离弃！老推敲客户的投诉动机乃肤浅行为。绝无太多被诬告之理！

　　The success of the service industry depends on everyone's attention to "services"! The essence is serving customers with a sincere attitude! The harder customers' requirements can be met, the more help we should offer, and the more prominent FORWARD will be. Frequent exculpation for yourself and your peers will drive away customers! And single-minded guess of customer's intention of complaint is actually superficial activities! The customers certainly have no reason to bring a false charge against you.

　　物流业必定打团体战，要取胜必须有团结心。当中精粹不单体现于日常工作里，亦同时验证于公司组织的户外及群体活动内！既是天霖人就得铸塑天霖心：一颗内外兼顾、四季同春的"团队雄心"！

　　The success of the logistics industry depends on the teamwork spirit. The essence does not only embody in daily work but also in outdoor and group activities organized by the company! Now that you are a staff at FORWARD, you shall have a "FORWARD-heart", a permanent ambitious teamwork heart caring for both internal and external!

企业信息化、情报化乃致胜要诀：可收抢先、突击、以小获大之效！多主动收集及分析市场、本部甚而与公司相关的动态来协调各部打赢胜仗才叫本事大；闭门造车者能逞什么英雄！

The essence to have a success is enterprise informationalization. The company can take the lead in striking with the intention to win more with less effort! Its managers shall actively analyze the market and even the development tendency of its division and the whole company from collected information to harmonize every division to win in the competition. This is really strong capacity. Can a person be a true hero with a blind eye to the outside world?

经营之道贵乎财才兼得！人资错配或姑息或放任乃糟无可糟！商战的失误没有巧合或误会，只有现实与事实。要自我抓平衡点，勿一面倒的偏激处事、偏颇待人；应先自求对错得失！

The operation shall attach importance to both talents and finance! Improper use of talents or indulgence can't be worse any more! The faults in commercial competition shall not be caused by coincidence or misunderstanding, but only facts and realities. You shall not go to extremes when getting along with others or dealing with matters and shall examine your faults and losses first!

人生精彩、天霖志壮。工作上偶尔的失误，只要无伤大雅又不影响管理系统的，也不必过于介怀！最怕错而不改、积非成是！天霖人需要面对更重要及有价值的事可多着呢！战事刚开始！

The life is wonderful, and FORWARD is ambitious. You shall not care about sporadic faults at work, if such faults don't matter much nor affect the management system! We are only afraid of cling to the mistake in stead of correcting it or getting used to what is wrong and regarding it as right! FORWARD people still have to treat with more important and more valuable things, and the competition has just begun!

　　经历多年奋战，从无到有、从有到急速壮大，有赖新旧仝仁的亦步亦趋！集团快将乔迁，誓再创"神话"：压力、挑战、牺牲，在所难免…神话面前、人人平等！

　　The inception and fast development of FORWARD shall thank for every staff's years of persistent efforts! The group is scheduled to remove to another place and to re-create the "myth"!Pressure, challenge and sacrifice will be unavoidable. Everyone is equal before the myth!

集团公司再次被评为Ａ级诚信企业：是团结成就大业的印证！相关主管全力抢滩，后勤与风险部门更不容松懈。戒骄戒燥、自强不息同庆贺！

The FORWARD group is entitled A-grade credit enterprise. It is the verification of its accomplishment upon comity! Relevant managers strain every nerve to snatch the market and the logistics & risks division also allows no relaxation. And every staff guards against arrogance and rashness and constantly strives to become stronger. The honor belongs to everyone!

天降甘霖，泽披物流先驱者；
恩逢雨露，福惠货代有心人！
God Bestows a Timely Rain,
and Benefits Logistics Vanguards;
God Bestows a Favour,
and Benefits Prepared Freight Forwarders.

温情篇

The Chapter on "Tender Loving Care"

　　天霖新时代，是汰弱留强的时候了！人贵自知、自量、自强不息求突破！切忌自我、自恃、自以为是轻进步！何所恃？功龄、学历、关系、才华？用人惟材啊！

　　The new era for FORWARD is the time for eliminating the weak and retaining the strong! A person is wise to know his limitations, estimate his own ability, and constantly strive to achieve breakthrough! He shall not be self-centered, self-relied or self-righteous. Self-righteousness is lead to small advancement. What do you rely on, age, degree, relationship or talent? Use staff in accordance with their talents!

　　闲时抱平常心享受假日休闲毋自寻烦恼；忙时用超强斗心推前浪，迈开新步伐。"天霖斗心"乃一视同仁，遇强愈强，无新旧人员之分。无业绩者、停滞不前者得注意了！

　　Enjoy holidays with normal attitude and never bring vexation on yourself when free; advance farther with strong ambition and take new steps when busy. "FORWARD-ambition" is treating equally without discrimination, becoming stronger after being strong and making no distinguishment between old and new staff. Those achieving no performance or no advancement should pay attention!

　　不断腾飞的企业让管理者创造锻炼与发展机会；既充实又累，但肯定有价值；夕阳企业绝对轻松自在，但未必会有明天！两者得失利弊，悉随尊便！

　　An emerging enterprise creates opportunities for managers to grow up and develop! Managers may feel substantial and tired, while are really worthy! They may feel relaxed and cozy at a sun-setting enterprise while will unnecessarily has a bright future! Ponder over the losses and gains as well as advantages and disadvantages, and choose whatever you like!

天寒地冻！当你饱尝热气腾腾的火锅或轻嚼美味的川菜时，别忘了一批为天霖、为你部打拼的前线人员！路遥知耐力，越见天霖心！美好的将来在眼前！

When you are tasting reeky chafing dish or chewing delicious Sichuan cuisine when the weather is cold and the ground is frozen, do not forget a batch of staffs who are working at the front line for FORWARD! As distance tests a person's persistence, so time reveals a FORWARD staff's heart! A bright future is just within our grasp!

　　狗年将临，善用这三十天先调整心态、手法，能跟上就是赢家：内部提速磨合、对外促销揽货；沉着面对市场变化、积极强化内部管理；广结善缘、少结怨。准没错！

　　The year of dog draws near. Please make good use of these 30 days to adjust your attitudes and methods. If you can catch up with the development tendency, you will become the winner. Interiorly, you shall be more harmonious with others. Exteriorly, you shall promote products and canvass goods actively. You shall also stay calm in the face of any market change and actively intensify the internal management. Make more friends and less enemies, and you will not miss it.

　　生活的波澜、工作的挫折，是上天赋予的磨炼，是福气！过多的顺遂、奢侈，乃上天设计的陷阱！自强不息、择善固执、孕育谦厚的内涵，才算真正的、持久的成功！谁也抢不走。

　　The ups and downs in the life as well as the setbacks at work are anneal and lucky given by the God! Over extravagance is a trap designed by the God! Constantly striving to become stronger, choosing what is good and following it, and cultivating hypocritically modest connotation are real and long-lasting success!

快乐、满足，因人而异。生活及工作上的烦恼、压力，多源于自己的心魔作祟。忍一时未必每次风平浪静，但退一步则肯定海阔天空，心境舒畅！

Happiness and satisfaction vary from person to person. The vexation and pressure in life and work usually arise from your evil emotion. You will be unnecessarily calm if you tolerate temporarily, while you will certainly feel comfortable if you recede a pace!

　　人谁无错！过去是记忆，以后是目标！小聪明得以发挥必成大智慧，真诚无价又无敌；不断的进步才显自身应有的价值。要培养敏锐的洞察与判断力来取代过感、过激与过虑的思维。

　　Nobody always do right! The past is the memory and the future is the aim! Petty trick will certainly become great wisdom of sincere, invaluable and invincible if it is brought into play. Continuous advancement embodies your deserved value. Try to cultivate your acute insight and sense to replace your sensitive, extreme and overworried thinking.

　　工作充满机遇、压力与挑战，是人生的写照！一时的得意必须持之以恒、再求突破；偶尔的失意乃锻炼心态与处事手法的良机！一息尚存则仍可改进。只怕执意自我钻死胡同内！

　　The work is full of opportunities, pressures and challenges and is the portraiture of the life! Temporary exultation is a chance to persevere and to break through, while unmeant chill is an opportunity to practise attitudes and ways for treating matters! Where there is life, there is chance of improvement. We are only afraid of getting into a dead end.

礼貌、服务或自我减压的基本功在于"笑"：一笑泯千愁！有见过苦着脸或装酷者被评为美丽、好看？微笑总比不笑好！

The basic skill for manners, services or self-relaxation is to "smile". A single smile keeps woes away! Have you ever seen anyone with a bitter face or pretension to be cool considered beautiful or good-looking? Smile is always better than none!

　　对尽责的主管来说，全天候的监督固然重要，可适当的运动、恰当的心灵放松尤为迫切。切勿自找烦扰，成为全天候的"压力奴隶"。去放松吧！

　　As for a responsible manager, all-day-long supervision is important, while proper exercise and appropriate relaxation are more exigent. Do not borrow trouble or become a round-the-clock slave for pressure. Just go to relax!

　　小年刚过，一周后就到春节了！"一年之计在于春"，你好趁节前认真反思今年礼貌、服务两项可有进步？现在部署，节后再励精图治则仍有"春暖花开结果时"！

　　The Spring Festival is to come in one week. "A year's plan starts with spring!" You shall take the chance to ponder over what advancements you have made in manners and services? Then make a plan. And make greater efforts after the spring festival. You will certainly gain more fruits!

年廿八，我帮你大扫除：敲你头，让你鸿运当头增智慧；插你眼，送你金睛玉眼看机遇；捅你鼻，赐你事事畅顺抢市场；掌你嘴，令你笑口常开善表达；扭你耳，教你广纳四面八方财；槌你心，要你心想事成人敦厚；咬你手，令你横财就手袋里塞；踩你腿，叫你一世丰足效率高；还有，拔你头发，帮你发上发！怕没!？

On December 28 of the last month prior to the upcoming Chinese New Year, I help you clean the house and know on wood to bless your wisdom. I touch your eyes to bless your ability to seize every opportunity. I poke your nose to bestow your good luck in seizing the market. I beat your mouth to wish you happiness and expressivity. I pull your ears to teach you to collect money everywhere. I beat your heart to wish you success and sincerity. I bite your hands to wish you more prize. I trample your leg to wish you high efficiency. And I draw your hair to wish you more wealth.

172

　　2006年首日金光遍大地、天霖显丰姿！象征成功、富贵、显达、团结和谐的一年！凡天霖人皆获天道庇佑，阖家欢畅。验证了"中央程式监控管理委员会"发布的天气预报：新的一年我们将遇到金钱雨、福瑞风、浓情雾、健康露、吉祥云、顺利霜、美满雷……和风旭日，财帛九州！它们将会围绕我们一整年，准备好了吗？让它们来得更猛烈些吧！！

　　On the first day of 2006, the world is covered by golden sunshine, and FORWARD is showing its charm! It is a year of success, richness, comity and harmoniousness! The God bless all FORWARD staff joyousness. It proves what the Central Quality Control Committee predicts: we will welcome wealth, fortune, tenderness, health, auspice, prosperity and happiness in the year of 2006! Moderate breeze, rising sun and wealth will surround us in the whole year. Are you ready? Just let these things come with more violence!

　　大年初五，抖擞精神、调整心态面对人、物、事。心宽，路自然宽；心开，自然活得有价值，哪怕世事变幻！心窄，得不偿失，咎由自取。

　　On the fifth day of Chinese New Year, re-energize your spirit and adjust your attitudes towards people, things and matters! A wide mind, a wide road! Wide mind naturally make you worthy, even though the affairs of the world change! Narrow mind makes the loss outweigh the gain and only brings troubles!

情人佳节，又是一个令人神驰、思忆纷呈的日子！南方降甘霖，北方见雨露，春回大地！不妨分点爱给天霖、给同僚、给客户；积极的要更积极，滞后固执的要洗心革面，迎接新机遇。全情投入可扭转人性弱点！

Valentines' Day is attractive and yearning! There is timely rain in the South and the North. Spring is here again! You might as well give some love to FORWARD, your peers and your customers! The active should be more active, and the sluggish and the bigoted shall reform thoroughly to get ready to welcome new opportunities. Total involvement in love can change your weakness!

　　"五一"是一个值得纪念的日子：集团乔迁、进口货量翻倍、关务的理性调整、销售策略的攻坚、信息工程部的良性突破、各后勤部门的积极投入，得大于失！得者莫喜，戒骄戒躁；失者莫悲，咎由自取！

　　"Labor Day" is worth memorizing! The group removed to a new place. Its revenue doubled. Public relations were adjusted reasonably. Sales strategy was implemented smoothly. The information technology division made new breakthroughs. The logistics division performed actively. And the group gained much and lost little! Nevertheless, the winner shall not be overdelighted and shall guard against arrogance; while the loser shall not be overdepressed or only have themselves to blame.

　　端午节的由来乃纪念屈原的"忠义"！祝愿天霖人以忠立于业内、以义证于同侪，自强不息！为自己、下属、亲人，努力再努力！端午节快乐！

　　Dragon Boat Festival is to commemorate especially the death of Qu Yuan, a great patriot poet who is said to have committed suicide by drowning himself in a river! Wish every FORWARD staff loyalty to their business, continuous self-renewal and endeavor for the sake of themselves, their subordinates, and relatives! Happy Dragon Boat Festival!

炎炎夏日必有雨露滋润，万物得以蓬勃茁长，此乃自然定律！做人、处事何尝不是？必须自我平衡，则成功在望！然高温令人烦躁，试多喝水，多怀关爱宽恕心，会发现"心善自然凉"，管用！

There are rains to moisten the world in sweltering summer. Therefore, everything on earth can grow flourishingly. This is a natural law! It is also suitable for the ways to get along with others and to treat with matters! Success will within your grasp, if you keep homeostatic! High temperature frets people. Try to drink more water and to be more concerned and remissive, you will find that you will be calm, cool and collected, when you are kind-hearted.

九月大革新，洗心又革面：轻率的我走了，正如我重新开始；我挥一挥狠劲，誓赶走一切劣性。害虫不再瞎鸣，天霖重获雨露！

September is a month for making a thorough reformation. My elimination of flippancy just gives me a new beginning. I make up my mind to drive away all bad habits. The disturber does no harm any more, and FORWARD regains its favor!

十月黄金周可让你稍作舒缓，亦同时静思得失；真正的绩效考核战幔亦随之打开，让你见证新时代之诞生。

You shall meditate gains and losses while enjoying appropriate relaxation during the National Day holiday. The real performance appraisal is to start to let you witness the birth of a new era.

普天同乐庆团圆, 甘霖皎月贺中秋; 勤有功, 诚见效; 同登顶峰再造极!
中秋节快乐!

All Chinese celebrate the traditionally Mid-Autumn Festival in bright moonlight. Diligence makes difference and honesty makes effect. FORWARD seeks glory after glory! Happy Mid-Autumn Festival!

金秋送爽，乍暖还寒，正是体悟人生好时节：积极肯定充实，认真绝对成事，困难就是磨炼；点点烛火可燎原亦可御寒发光。要善用智慧！

The golden autumn is the best time for appreciating the life. Activity makes you feel enriched. Earnestness unnecessarily leads to success. And setbacks are to temper yourself! Candlelight can set the prairie ablaze, protect against cold and illuminate! Please make good use of your wisdom!

　　最佳的圣诞礼物乃学会"人贵自知"！当你认为已鹤立鸡群，排众而出，或岗位没人可替，或瞒天过海、没人吭声时，你已亮红灯警报了！没有解决不了的难题，更没有孤芳自赏的持久成功者！

　　The best present for Christmas is the good understanding of your advantages and shortcomings! When you stand head and shoulders above others or practice deception, you may receive a warning! There is no problem that can't be solved. A man who is indulging in self-admiration can never be a permanent success man.

经过长假后重投战阵总觉力不从心,有点压力吧! 不妨先冷静五分钟后,用纸笔把未来十五天该完成的事记下来,再喝口水、洗洗手后即启动你的天霖斗心跟进!

You may found that your strength falls short of your desire or you have come under some pressure when putting into work after the long holiday! Try to calm down for five minutes and write down the things you have to finish in the following 15 days. Then have a drink and wash your hands to start your chase with an "ambitious FORWARD-heart".

　　星期天，该休息时好好休息，该放松时要放松；勿忘抽丁点时间遥控你部！除非你肯定下属已然超卓并学会主动汇报？

　　Just rest and relax on Sunday. Don't forget to spend some time acquainting yourself with subordinates within your division, unless you believe they have been extremely excellent and have learned to report to you initiatively!

　　高层主管处事以"公司利益"为前提、中层及前线主管处事亦以"公司利益"为前提！天霖家里个人的吵闹荣辱视等闲。有完美丰盛的家才有丰足的天霖人啊！

　　High-level managers shall give priority to the company's interest when treating with matters. The medium- and lower-level managers shall also obey this principle! Arguments, disputes, honors or disgraces within the FORWARD family are all unimportant. There aren't affluent FORWARD people unless there is a perfect FORWARD family!

天降甘霖，泽披物流先驱者；
恩逢雨露，福惠货代有心人！
God Bestows a Timely Rain,
and Benefits Logistics Vanguards;
God Bestows a Favour,
and Benefits Prepared Freight Forwarders.

天霖七剑三棍篇

The Legend of FORWARD Seven Swords

武学秘笈
Secret of success

凡我门生必读，耳濡目染，代代传授下去……
All FORWARD staff must learn this with no hesitation

七剑传说

远古传说，江湖变幻，道消魔长，幸有天山七剑降妖除魔，匡扶正义，日渐天下太平，国富民强，七剑隐退江湖……

日光斗转，世纪迭换，传闻七剑重现黄土大地。时值乙酉年九月初六午时，天上七色祥云乍现，紫气弥漫！群豪低首、百兽俯伏！期待神兵降临……

——是七剑！七剑已然重临……乾坤昭日月、流水行云会天晖、赤电映玄武、潜龙傲啸青月舞，七剑现天霖！

Here comes the lengend……

Once upon a time, there was a Dark Dynasty crowded with evils, crimes, decays and deaths. Notwithstanding how gloomy it was, the FORWARD SEVEN SWORDS strived hard to completely eliminate these wrongs, and with much effort, a peaceful and healthy society lasted for years.

As time went by, the society was again attacked by sinful act and affected the lives of various civilians. Dark shadow was cast over everyone, leaving them with no hope and prospect for the future. What they could do was to pray and hope that miracles would come.

In the year of October 2005, people suddenly found sunshine through the rain. Rainbow dazzled everyone's eyes. The FORWARD SEVEN SWORDS appeared again. Having the mission to control, empower and re-engineer, the seven swords became one and is now known as the FORWARD SOVEREIGN SWORD, a unique one dominating the field and striving ahead to be the leader in China where further success stories continue.

Let us have a look at the characteristics of the 7 swords……

乾坤日月剑的特点

剑分阴阳，精光内敛，含天地乾坤正气；攻守兼备，进退有序，主贵；善深入敌后，逆转乾坤制胜；剑本具皇者之风，为剑中之首；惟铸炼过程中因日月精华失衡，令其偶尔相互牵制，无法充分驾驭；剑心曾受过多的月精华孕育而稍欠锐气！

The Heaven and Earth Sword

The sword itself had two separate pieces with two complementary principles in nature, serving wide range of aspects. It should be the best among the swords. However, the core of the sword was a bit over-done in casting, affecting its judgment in achieving total satisfaction.

流云剑的特点

剑中有剑，相辅相成！剑身似重实轻，灵巧飘逸有致，勇谋兼备，主智；善稳守突击，穿插敌阵丛中寻隙杀敌，一举制胜；惟久历战阵，剑心向善，未免忽视江湖俗气，稍有浮夸而易被敌人乘虚而入！

The Soaring Sword

The sword appeared heavy, yet it was actually light. It contained two back-up daggers fighting swiftly and always performed unexpected attacks with special effects. However, it was sometimes frivolous, a downside that could lead to the opportunity-seizing by its opponent.

天晖剑的特点

剑身迸发耀目光华，仁爱双修、刚柔并济，遇事以大无畏精神奋勇抗敌，乃天道正宗，主富；善谋划，匡扶正气，杀敌于无形；惟剑心偏软且傲，易陷敌网，自招困恼。

The Splendor Sword

The sword had a splendid outlook and a high level of competence. It was renowned for its outstanding natural life-span and its imperceptible high achievement capability. Yet, its supercilious reaction could sometimes lead to troubles.

赤电剑的特点

外刚内柔之剑！剑身迸发刚阳之气，既虚似实，三分攻七分守，主忠；善后援维护，杀敌时有若电击之势；惟剑心虽逞强势，难掩其阴柔护短之剑意，易自伤其身。

The Velocity Sword

Being the heaviest sword with two separate unique swords merged together, it acted as a vanguard and gave out roaring victorious sound during fights against others. Save for, its casualness sometimes blocked its way to accomplish perfect missions.

玄武剑的特点

刚阳之剑！剑身以玄铁铸造，一分为二，开合有劲，剑出有虎啸雷鸣之势，主勇；善冲锋陷阵，杀敌于弹指之间 ；惟剑心稍欠历炼而不免流于脆弱，易生只攻不守之弊、易犯孤高之险！

The Thunder Sword

The sword was claimed to have a conservative core, specializing in defense and upholding the rights and principles for the rest of the swords. Acting as a thunderer to scare and break through barriers, the sword seemed to lack attention to the way it attacked. The way it shielded a shortcoming or fault sometimes caused internal conflicts among the team.

潜龙剑的特点

剑身实而不华，乃忠直之剑；动如龙在九天，静若潜龙在野，主义；善攻略，进退有度，扰敌制胜；惟剑心于精钢铸炼时过火而致刚毅有余、阴柔不足，稍欠灵巧易自生魔障……

The Devotion Sword

The sword was always dedicated to success. It could be adapted to both active and passive trends in integrations of the overall situation. However, its firm and persistent approach would sometimes become frailness especially dealing with calamity.

青月剑的特点

　　剑身轻柔带青黄气，随风而变，时隐时现，主巧；善孤剑入阵，飘忽杀敌后遁没；惟铸剑过程中剑身曾受损，虽经愈合已令剑心受创，杀敌时稍欠灵活变阵，易生枝节，自堕罗网。

The Misty Sword

　　The sword was a unique one performing tasks independently with good results, especially for those with foundation and experience. However, its unsociable and eccentric nature would easily be isolated and this affected it to take advantage of the favorable circumstances towards victory.

后记

七剑各有千秋、各具特色，必须取长补短，七剑合一方显最大威力！然江湖险恶、风云变幻、能人辈出、强敌环伺，要一举得天下，就得同时发挥"天霖三绝棍"的神髓，融会贯通，方可尽显七剑之精华，铸就无坚不摧、分金断石、战无不胜、攻无不克的皇者之剑——天霖皇道剑——气吞天下，一统江湖……

Postscript

As the seven swords consisted of respective strengths and weaknesses, it was mandatory that each and every one of them to team-up complementarily in order to maximize gains. In addition to having good team spirits, the 7 swords must all profoundly harbor simultaneously and be in line with the FORWARD THREE SUPER RODS. This was crucial for them to become the irreplaceable leader which could dominate the field from generation to generation.

天霖三绝棍
The FORWARD Three Super Rods

天心棍（心态调整棍）
亦刚亦柔如行云流水，松柏精神，审时度势，发挥忘我智慧灭心魔。

The Talent Rod
It could perform self-appraisal and self-proceed with remedial actions to eliminate its own weaknesses and cope with changing crisis. There was no ceiling in its life cycle.

天财棍（开源节流棍）

无私奉献，灵活调配，主动发掘江湖宝藏，节约粮草，防患未然，兼收并蓄；扶战友，歼外敌。

The Gold Foil Rod

It was capable to explore opportunities in reducing cost as well as maximizing profit margin for long term expansion. Adequate and sufficient resources were tailor-made for the appropriate era.

天灵棍（灵动棍）

　　洞悉天机，内外兼控，回避江湖风险时亦勇于面对内部流弊；做到运筹帷幄，决胜千里之外。

The Inspirational Rod

It could forecast, augur and take precautions against various risk aspects. One of its critical success factors that it had was to turn experience into knowledge and techniques.

七剑三棍传奇之终极篇
The Ultimate Goals

天霖皇道剑

乃七剑会三棍的精华所在，气吞天下，惟剑独尊！其剑意：乾门添正将，坤宅显吉祥，流芳传百代，潜心可见性，青风拂善人，天道悯众生，赤胆忠义情，玄天共表证，剑啸冲凌霄，心藏浩然气，财帛冠九州，灵犀达四方，棍剑合一心，皇者独天霖！

凡我门生必须勤练七剑三棍之精髓，祈早集"天霖皇道剑"之大成，从点到面，转化为立体持续动力，寻空隙，破旧弊，抢占先机，生生不息……则天霖得天下，不远矣！

POSTSCRIPT -THE FORWARD SOVEREIGN SWORD

The Forward Seven Swords and the Forward Three Super Rods could be exclusively twinkled on different tasks but they cannot always carry out full-house success.

Their blemishes could only be rectified and reformed through team efforts and aligned harmony so as to extract and purify an exquisite fine arts. The FORWARD SOVEREIGN SWORD, the combination of the 7 swords, and the 3 super rods, is therefore held in high-esteem. This sword can be finally composed and dominates the field completely with radiant reputation. Nothing can replace the FORWARD SOVERIGN SWORD as it is definitely a legend that possesses all excellences and superiorities.

Let us celebrate the "Forward Dynasty" appearing on stage......

天降甘霖，泽披物流先驱者；
恩逢雨露，福惠货代有心人！
God Bestows a Timely Rain,
and Benefits Logistics Vanguards;
God Bestows a Favour,
and Benefits Prepared Freight Forwarders.

附录

Appendices

天霖国际货运集团简介

　　天霖国际货运集团是一家实力雄厚、信誉昭著的跨国集团公司，总部位于中国香港特别行政区，辖下四十二家子公司遍布各地。集团全体仝仁锐意进取、开拓创新，经过多年的持续发展，形成以物流运输、仓储配套、物流软件开发为主导，项目投资、餐饮连锁及贸易服务等广泛领域的综合化经营体系。

　　天霖国际货运集团致力于中国物流市场的拓展已达十个年头；其间，集团紧随中国的经济发展及战略步伐，深谙中国物流市场之发展规律，对培育行业力量、构建物流网络、繁荣地区经济不遗余力，在新的年度里，集团将重点开发天霖神州物流联盟项目，致力打造中国人主导的优质物流品牌，为天霖的特许商务伙伴创造丰硕的成果！

Corporate Introduction

FORWARD Group Logistics & Transportation Limited is a transnational corporation with powerful strength and impeccable reputation. Headquartered in Hong Kong Special Administration Region of China, it has 42 subsidiaries under its wings. With all members keen to advance and innovate, the group has formed a comprehensive operation system with dominant focus on logistics related business, storage counterpart and the development of logistics software and broad coverage of an array of fields, such as project investment, chain restaurants and trading services, which has become well known in the field.

FORWARD Group Logistics & Transportation Limited has committed itself to developing the Chinese logistics market for ten years. During the past years, it has been closely following China's economic development and strategic change. Acquainted itself with the development law of the Chinese logistics market, it spared no effort to cultivating its influence in the logistics industry, building a complete logistics network and prospering regional economy. In the year of 2007, the company will lay an emphasis on "FORWARD Logistics Alliance" and make great efforts to build an excellent Chinese-dominant logistics brand and to create fruitful results for FORWARD's business partners!

天霖屡获殊荣　物流天之骄子

天霖国际货运集团是一家实力雄厚的跨国集团公司,以其优质的物流服务蜚声中外,饮誉全球,屡获国家、行业及社会的相关单位及机关认可。

＊ 国家单位授予的殊荣

首家荣获中港政府 CEPA 政策批准成立之国家一级货运代理企业

首家荣获中港政府授权经营之无缝连接—绿色通道跨境物流企业

中国物流最具影响力品牌

中国十佳货代企业

中国十佳快运快递企业

中国十佳物流配送企业

中国物流民营企业 100 强

中国对外贸易理事会理事单位

全国服务诚信示范单位称号

中国创新优秀企业荣誉单位

中国产学研联合促进会理事单位

＊ 行业机关授予的殊荣

深圳机场海关评为 A 类诚信企业

深圳机场检验检疫局评为 A 级诚信企业

中国邮政总局授权代理,特许经营350G 以下文件、包裹,不受现有的政策限制

中国民航总局指定的航空货物代理

中国航空运输业协会副会长单位

深圳市物流协会副会长单位

＊ 社会团体授予的殊荣

ISO9000:2000 国际质量体系认证

世界华人企业家协会理事单位

香港中小企业总会主管单位

青岛天霖物流培训学院荣誉主管单位

深圳市外商投资协会副会长单位

深圳市优秀外资企业

FORWARD's Prizes & Credits

FORWARD Group Logistics & Transportation Limited has been recognized by the country, the industry and the society, as follows.

* Governmental Authorities-Awarded Credits
* The First National First-grade Freight Forwarding Enterprise established under CEPA
* The First Seamless Connection-Green Channel- Cross-border Logistics Enterprise authorized by the China-Hong Kong Government
* The Most Influential Logistics Brand in China
* China's Top 10 Freight Forwarding Enterprises
* China's Top 10 Express Enterprises
* China's Top 10 Logistics Delivery Enterprises
* China's Top 100 Private Logistics Enterprises
* Board Member of The Council of China's Foreign Trade
* Award of National Demonstrative Entity for Service Credit
* Honorable Entity of Chinese Excellent Innovation Enterprises
* Board Member of China Federation of Industries & Research Insitution
* Industrial Organs-Awarded Credits
* Class A Credit Enterprise awarded by Shenzhen Airport Customs
* Class A Enterprise awarded by Shenzhen Airport Entry-Exit Inspection and Quarantine Bureau
* Authorised Agent of The State Post Bureau of China with no restriction in operating courier shipments weighing less than 350 gram
* Authorised Agent of The Civil Aviation Administration of China (CAAC)
* Board Member of China Air Transport Association
* Board Member of Shenzhen Logistics Association
* Social Communities-Awarded Credits
* ISO9000£∫2000 International Quality Management System Certification
* Board Member of The World Chinese Entrepreneurs Association
* Board Member of Hong Kong S & M Enterprises General Association (HKSMEGA)
* Board Member of Forward Logistics Management (Qingdao) Institute
* Board Member of Shenzhen Association of Enterprises with Foreign Investment
* Excellent Foreign-funded Enterprise in Shenzhen

集团公司使命

　　天霖集团全体员工一致承诺，遵照集团一贯的优良企管及营运策略，上下一心，以客为尊，致力为公司创建优质品牌，为客户提供高效服务，携手并进，共同缔造佳绩，营造出高度的经济效益；借此，我们已誓师出发，主动出击，誓要严加把关，内外配合，不断的提升服务质量，永远地驱动潮流，高瞻远瞩，不辞劳苦，迈开远大的步伐，朝全球性、全方向型的经营方针奋进；我们要全力拼搏，再创新峰！

Misson Statement

　　We are toally committed to the Company's Service-Returns-Prospect (S-R-P) philosophy. We will provide superior tailored services to our customers and work closely with our strategic partners, so as to produce outstanding financial. Returns and achieve long-term success. Being at the beginning of this new century in China , we are ready and well equipped to strengthen controls and continuously improve our overall service standard to ensure that we are always the role Model of the industry.

　　With the effective re-invention, strong teamwork and dedication of each staff, our industry leader position will maintain and our success will definitely go beyond Greater China.

行政管理方针

1.以人为本：尊重每一员工之重要性。

2. 服务为先：100% 全情投入，维持"满分"形象。

3.利润回馈：群策群力，争取最大利润，以便反馈员工，同步前进。

4.汰弱留强：全面实施"精兵制"，宁缺毋滥，全力拼搏。

5.公私分明：推广公司政策予各阶层的员工，使发挥群体合作精神，而凝聚整体团结力量。

6.选贤任能：首重内部培训，筛升优秀员工，取长补短。

7.灵活变通：新人事，新作风，随时作适当调整，绝不能坚持错误的决定。

8.开源节流：扩大营业额，节约开销，为员工创造美好的将来。

Company Strategy

1.People: Respect each staff & their contribution.

2.Service: 100% customer satisfaction.

3.Returns: Earn high returns for developing staff team & business.

4.Manpower: Maintain real contributors at different level.

5.Fairness: Apply company policies to all levels of staff to strengthen team spirit.

6.Recruiting£ʃ Focus on staff training and "Promote-from-within" policy.

7.Flexibility: Promote continuous change management.

8.Cost Control: Best resources utilization.

经营理念

　　集团公司凭借优良的作业系统，于中港及海外各分支机构，贯彻推行S-R-P行政管理理念。集团公司深信，只要坚定遵循企业经营宗旨，为客户提供超高水平的服务，自然地会循序渐进地得到合理之回报，只要公司全体员工团结互助，努力拼搏，公司将会不断发展，共创灿烂美好的未来。

Corporate Philosophy

S-R-P
S=Services　　服务
R=Returns　　回报
P=Prospects　前景

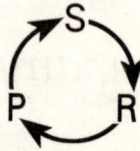

S-R-P are the principles that govern every FORWARD Group activity in china ,HongKong and her international network.

FORWARD Group deeply believes that to deliver impeccables service to our customers will reward us with good returns ,which will secure us a future of prosperity . The S-R-P Philosophy is an unbroken chain that up-holds the others and is supported by them.

风险管理架构图

风险监控管理的目的：运用各种技术手段及应对措施，确保公司的人员、货物及财产安全。

★ 为公司员工、交易客户创造安全、稳定的工作、营商环境；

★ 确保进出公司的货物无违禁、冒牌物品，重量、品名与实际相符；

★ 确保公司财产的安全，确保资金的回收，维护公司的合法权益不受侵害。

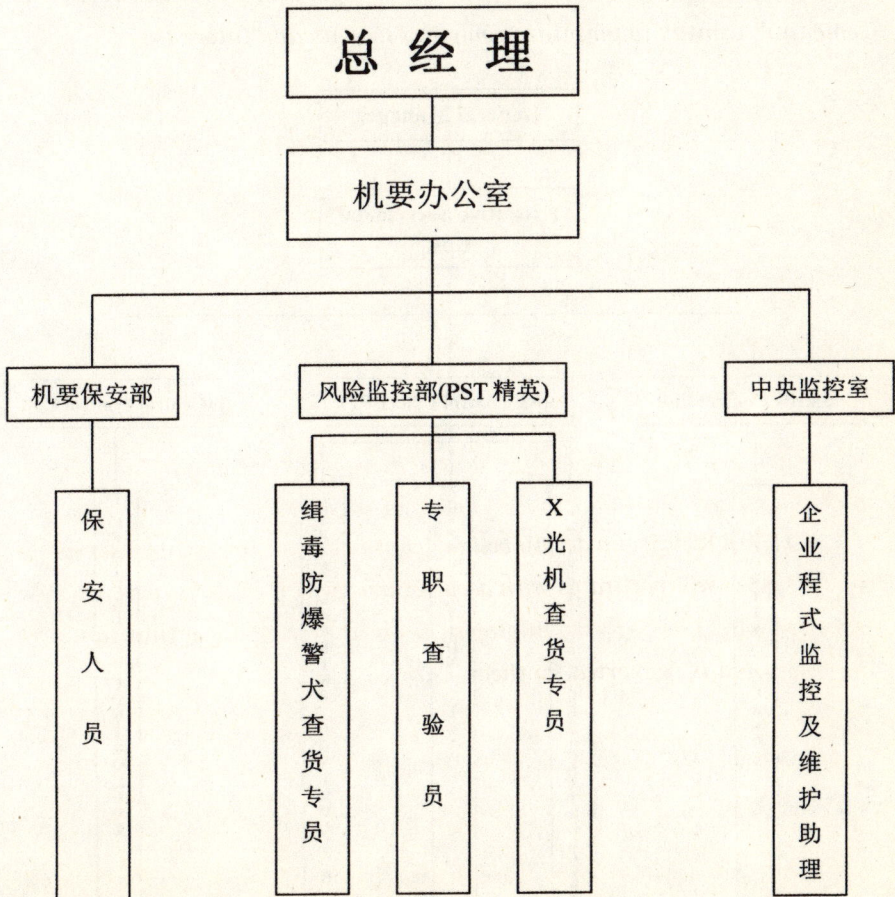

总经理

机要办公室

机要保安部　　风险监控部(PST 精英)　　中央监控室

保安人员　　缉毒防爆警犬查货专员　　专职查验员　　X光机查货专员　　企业程式监控及维护助理

Risk Control Chart
of FORWARD Group International Transportation Limited

AIM: With all kinds of technology and measures, to make sure the safety of our staff, goods and property.

★ To create a nice work & business environment for staff & customers;

★ To insure NO CONTRABAND & NO FAKER through Logistics Center; And make the same between shipment and their weight/type name;

★ To insure the safety of company's property and the return of company's capital; to maintain company's rights and interests;

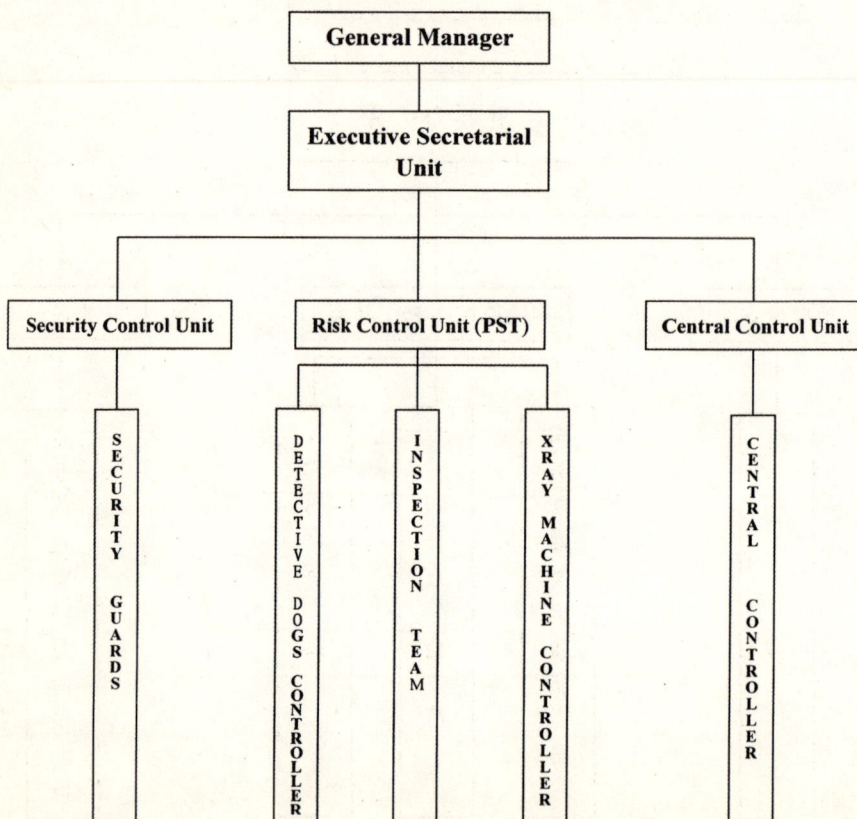

```
                        General Manager
                              |
                     Executive Secretarial
                             Unit
                              |
     ┌────────────────────────┼────────────────────────┐
Security Control Unit   Risk Control Unit (PST)    Central Control Unit
     |              ┌──────────┼──────────┐             |
  SECURITY      DETECTIVE  INSPECTION   XRAY         CENTRAL
   GUARDS      DOGS        TEAM       MACHINE      CONTROLLER
             CONTROLLER              CONTROLLER
```

风险监控流程图

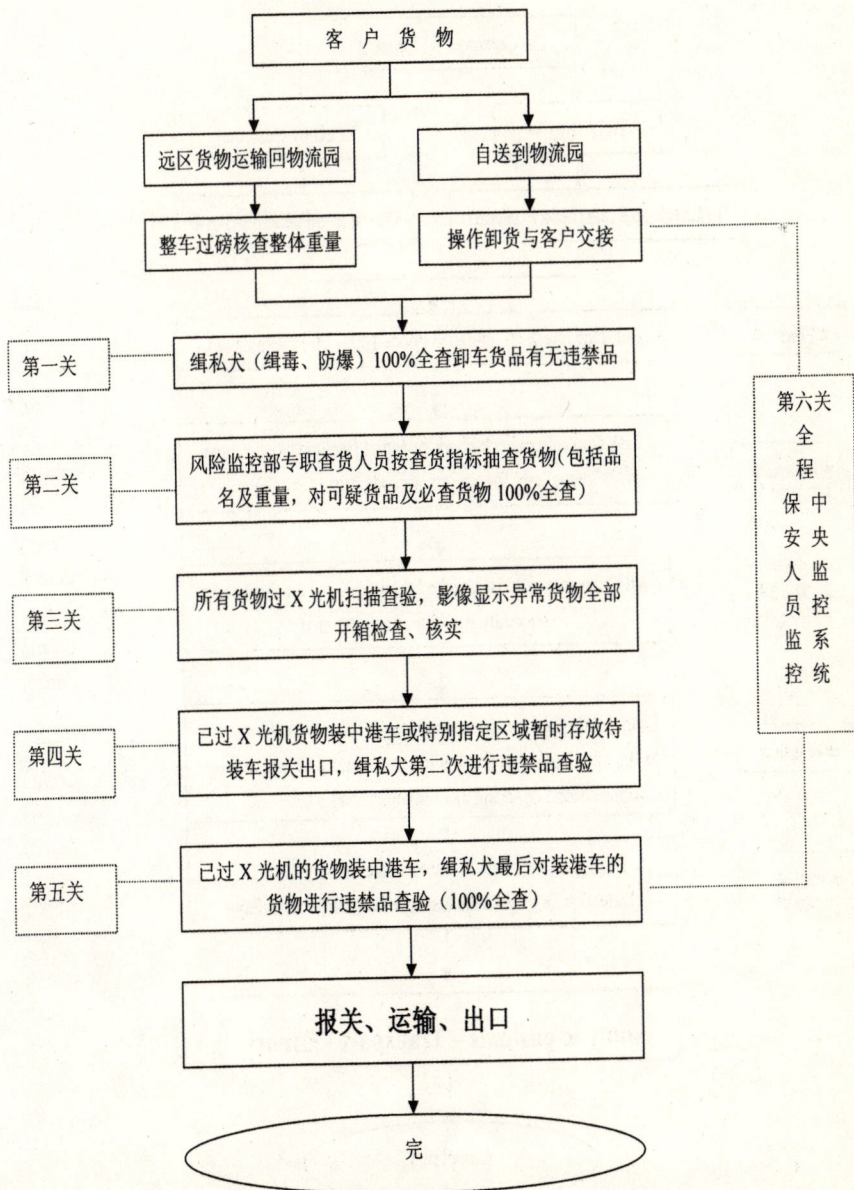

```
        ┌──────────────────┐
        │   客 户 货 物     │
        └──────────────────┘
                 │
        ┌────────┴─────────┐
        ▼                  ▼
┌──────────────┐   ┌──────────────┐
│远区货物运输回 │   │  自送到物流园 │
│  物流园      │   │              │
└──────────────┘   └──────────────┘
        │                  │
        ▼                  ▼
┌──────────────┐   ┌──────────────┐
│整车过磅核查整 │   │操作卸货与客户 │
│  体重量      │   │   交接       │
└──────────────┘   └──────────────┘
```

第一关	缉私犬（缉毒、防爆）100%全查卸车货品有无违禁品
第二关	风险监控部专职查货人员按查货指标抽查货物（包括品名及重量，对可疑货品及必查货物100%全查）
第三关	所有货物过X光机扫描查验，影像显示异常货物全部开箱检查、核实
第四关	已过X光机货物装中港车或特别指定区域暂时存放待装车报关出口，缉私犬第二次进行违禁品查验
第五关	已过X光机的货物装中港车，缉私犬最后对装港车的货物进行违禁品查验（100%全查）

第六关 全程保安人员监控 中央监控系统

报关、运输、出口

完

备注：凡查货发现违禁物品立即暂扣货物，并通报风险监控部主管处理退货事宜。

Risk Control Flow Chart

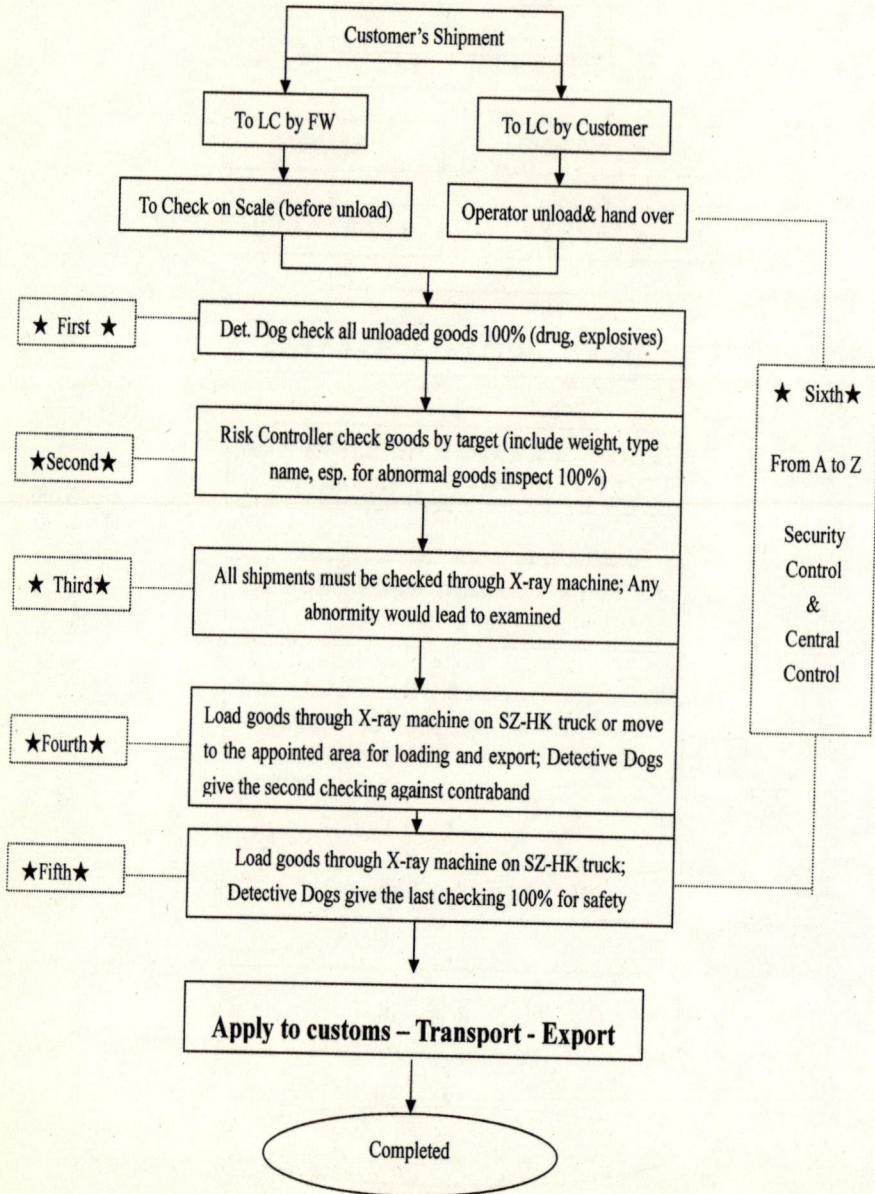

```
                    ┌─────────────────────────────┐
                    │     Customer's Shipment      │
                    └─────────────────────────────┘
              ┌──────────────────┐      ┌──────────────────┐
              │   To LC by FW    │      │ To LC by Customer│
              └──────────────────┘      └──────────────────┘
        ┌──────────────────────────────┐  ┌──────────────────────────────┐
        │ To Check on Scale (before unload)│  │ Operator unload& hand over │
        └──────────────────────────────┘  └──────────────────────────────┘
```

★ First ★ → Det. Dog check all unloaded goods 100% (drug, explosives)

★Second★ → Risk Controller check goods by target (include weight, type name, esp. for abnormal goods inspect 100%)

★ Third★ → All shipments must be checked through X-ray machine; Any abnormity would lead to examined

★Fourth★ → Load goods through X-ray machine on SZ-HK truck or move to the appointed area for loading and export; Detective Dogs give the second checking against contraband

★Fifth★ → Load goods through X-ray machine on SZ-HK truck; Detective Dogs give the last checking 100% for safety

★ Sixth★

From A to Z

Security
Control
&
Central
Control

Apply to customs – Transport - Export

(Completed)

Menu:Any contraband be checkeb out,it would de returned back by Rist Control Officer.

风险管理工作量化指标

一、缉私犬查验指标：100% 全部验货。

二、专职查验员查验指标：

1.整体查货率超过 50%；

2.对黑名单客户（之前有违禁记录）、付现金客户、新客户、送货上门客户 100% 查验；

3.X 光机扫描及缉私犬检查有异常货物 100% 查验；

4.饭店类（非固定办公地点）场所寄件、特定车次货物、特定航班货物、寄件人资讯不全货物 100% 查验；

5.密封货物、重量不均货物、触觉异常货物、有异味货物、货物内容与实际申报不符货物等情况进行 100% 查验；

三、X 光机扫描查验指标：100% 全部验货。

Risk Controlling Quality Target

1.Detective Dogs' Checking Target￡∫100%Examine all goods.

2.nspection Team's Checking Target:

a.The checking rate for all goods: more than 50%;

b.100% inspect these customers': Black Sheet/Cash Payment/New Customers/Sent goods to LC;

c.Any abnormal goods which was founded by X-Ray or Det.Dogs, would be given to examine 100% ;

d.100% inspect these articles: Sent by restaurant(no address)/Regular Time Truck or Flight/Shipper's info incomplete;

e.100% inspect as following: Sealed articles/unbalanced weight/touch abnormal/ Peculiar Smell/Unconformity between invoice and articles.

3.X-Ray Machine Checking Target￡∫100%Examine.

拒收物品表

货币（包括银行本票、汇票、支票、债券、股票）、易燃易爆品、军火武器及其零配件、仿真军火成品及其零配件、腐蚀品、液体、粉末状、赌博用具、鲜活物品、光／磁碟、宗教及政治宣传品、淫秽及色情物品、药品、烟草及酒精类、古董文物、珠宝首饰及贵金属、汽车零配件、冒名牌或侵产权物品、毒品、厚度在三公分以上的石板、打火机以及其它海关禁运之物品。

Items Not Acceptable

We do not accept transportation of money (including but not limited to coins, travelers checks or negotiable instrument equivalent to cash such as endorsed stocks and bonds),explosives, firearms, weaponry and their parts and imitation, perishable items, powder or liquid , gambling devices, foodstuffs, live animals and plants, VCD or disk, religionary & political throwaway, pornography, medicines, tobacco, alcoholic beverages, antiques, jewelry, previous metals, auto and auto parts stamps, faker, drug, lighter, flag, and all prohibited items restricted by IATA regulations.

成功案例 Success Stories

风险监控查获仿名牌运动服
Fake sport jackets

风险监控查获仿名牌鞋子
Fake sport shoes

风险监控查获疑似违禁药品
Mediciness

风险监控查获疑似违禁液体物品
Lquid items

风险监控查获疑似仿古董文物
Antiques

风险监控查获鞋垫内藏香烟及货币
Tobacco and money

风险监控查获疑似枪支配件
Firearms

风险监控查获一批盗版光碟
VCD & disk

贵重物品交接流程

一、远区贵重货物入仓

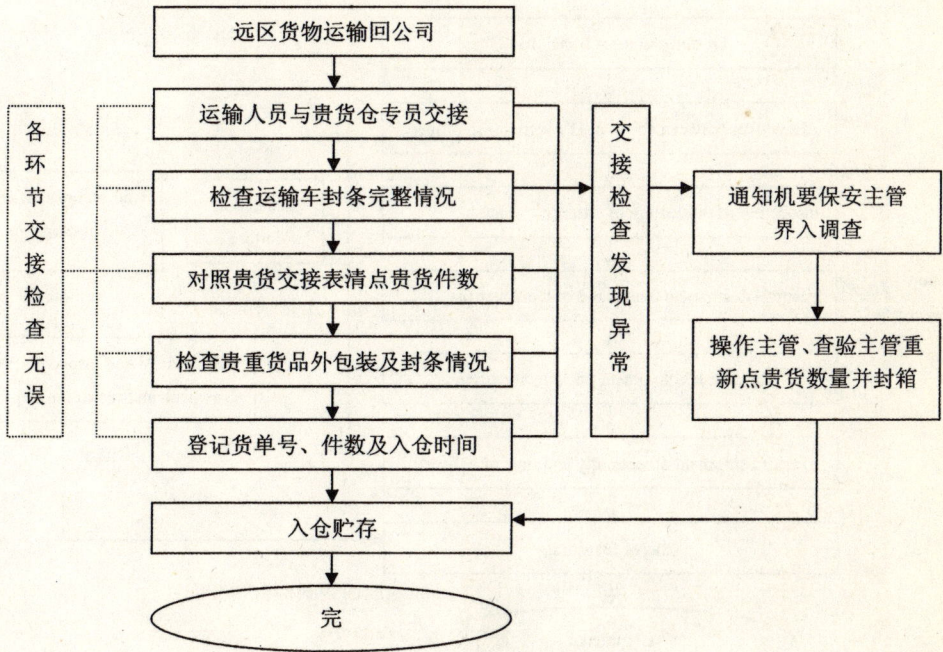

```
┌─────────────────────────────┐
│      远区货物运输回公司        │
└─────────────────────────────┘
              │
┌──────┐ ┌─────────────────────────────┐    ┌────────┐
│各     │ │    运输人员与贵货仓专员交接    │    │交       │
│环     │ └─────────────────────────────┘    │接       │
│节     │ ┌─────────────────────────────┐    │检       │   ┌─────────────────────┐
│交     │ │    检查运输车封条完整情况      │    │查       │   │  通知机要保安主管       │
│接     │ └─────────────────────────────┘    │发       │──▶│    界入调查           │
│检     │ ┌─────────────────────────────┐    │现       │   └─────────────────────┘
│查     │ │    对照贵货交接表清点贵货件数   │    │异       │              │
│无     │ └─────────────────────────────┘    │常       │   ┌─────────────────────┐
│误     │ ┌─────────────────────────────┐    │        │   │  操作主管、查验主管重   │
│       │ │   检查贵重货品外包装及封条情况  │    │        │   │  新点贵货数量并封箱     │
└──────┘ └─────────────────────────────┘    └────────┘   └─────────────────────┘
          ┌─────────────────────────────┐                          │
          │    登记货单号、件数及入仓时间   │                          │
          └─────────────────────────────┘                          │
                       │                                            │
          ┌─────────────────────────────┐                          │
          │          入仓贮存             │◀─────────────────────────┘
          └─────────────────────────────┘
                       │
                 (    完    )
```

High Value Shipment Handling Procedure

1. Distant HV Shipment to HV Warehouse

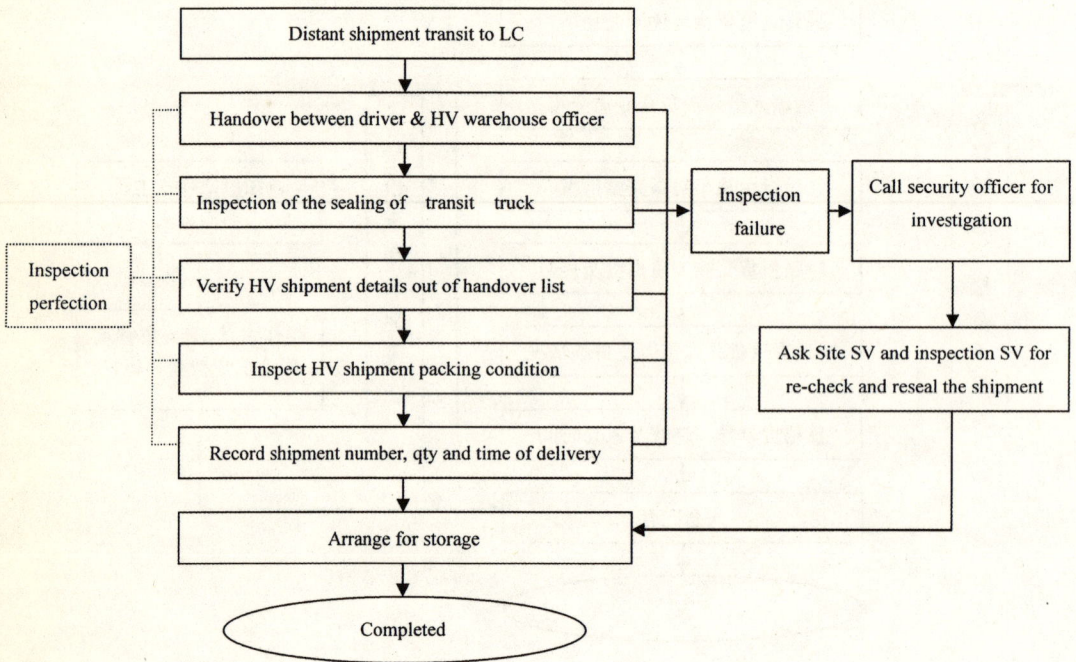

```
┌─────────────────────────────────────────┐
│        Distant shipment transit to LC     │
└─────────────────────────────────────────┘
                    │
                    ▼
┌─────────────────────────────────────────┐
│  Handover between driver & HV warehouse   │
│               officer                      │
└─────────────────────────────────────────┘
                    │
                    ▼
┌─────────────────────────────────────────┐        ┌──────────────┐       ┌─────────────────────┐
│  Inspection of the sealing of  transit    │───────▶│  Inspection  │──────▶│ Call security officer│
│              truck                         │        │   failure    │       │   for investigation  │
└─────────────────────────────────────────┘        └──────────────┘       └─────────────────────┘
                    │                                                                  │
                    ▼                                                                  ▼
┌─────────────────────────────────────────┐                          ┌─────────────────────────┐
│  Verify HV shipment details out of        │                          │ Ask Site SV and          │
│  handover list                             │                          │ inspection SV for        │
└─────────────────────────────────────────┘                          │ re-check and reseal the  │
                    │                                                   │ shipment                 │
                    ▼                                                   └─────────────────────────┘
┌─────────────────────────────────────────┐                                          │
│  Inspect HV shipment packing condition     │                                         │
└─────────────────────────────────────────┘                                          │
                    │                                                                  │
                    ▼                                                                  │
┌─────────────────────────────────────────┐                                          │
│  Record shipment number, qty and time of   │                                        │
│  delivery                                   │                                        │
└─────────────────────────────────────────┘                                          │
                    │                                                                  │
                    ▼                                                                  │
┌─────────────────────────────────────────┐◀─────────────────────────────────────────┘
│           Arrange for storage              │
└─────────────────────────────────────────┘
                    │
                    ▼
              ╭─────────────╮
              │  Completed   │
              ╰─────────────╯
```

Inspection perfection

二、客户送货上门贵重货物

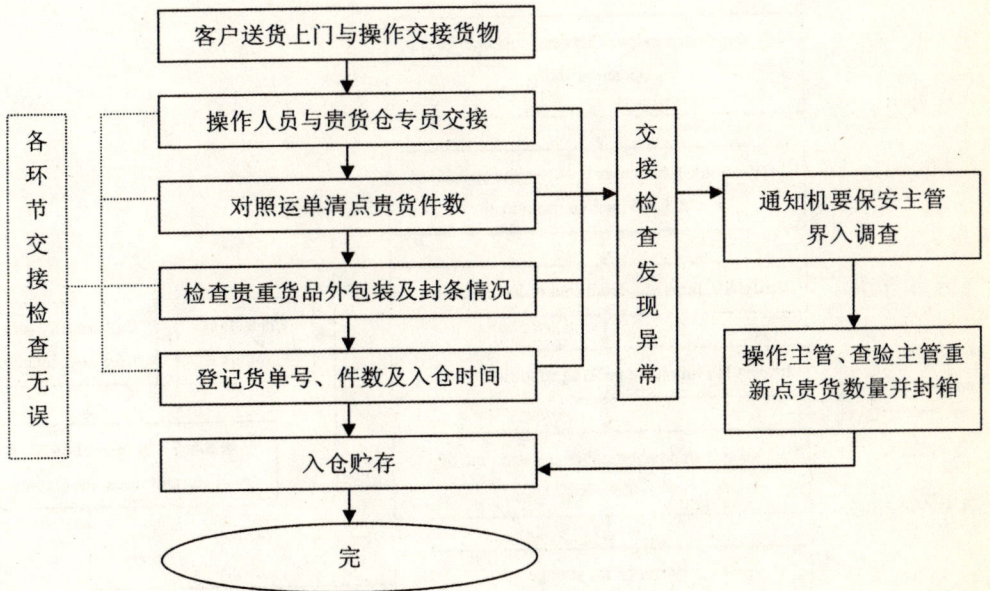

```
        ┌─────────────────────────┐
        │   客户送货上门与操作交接货物   │
        └─────────────────────────┘
                     ↓
  各   ┌─────────────────────────┐     ┌──────┐     ┌─────────────────┐
  环   │   操作人员与贵货仓专员交接   │     │ 交   │     │   通知机要保安主管   │
  节   └─────────────────────────┘     │ 接   │  →  │    界入调查       │
  交        ↓                          │ 检   │     └─────────────────┘
  接   ┌─────────────────────────┐     │ 查   │              ↓
  检   │   对照运单清点贵货件数      │  →  │ 发   │     ┌─────────────────┐
  查   └─────────────────────────┘     │ 现   │     │  操作主管、查验主管重   │
  无        ↓                          │ 异   │     │  新点贵货数量并封箱   │
  误   ┌─────────────────────────┐     │ 常   │     └─────────────────┘
       │   检查贵重货品外包装及封条情况 │     └──────┘              ↓
       └─────────────────────────┘
            ↓
       ┌─────────────────────────┐
       │   登记货单号、件数及入仓时间  │
       └─────────────────────────┘
            ↓
       ┌─────────────────────────┐
       │        入仓贮存          │  ←───────────────────────
       └─────────────────────────┘
            ↓
          （    完    ）
```

2. Accept HV Shipment from Customer Transit to HV Warehouse

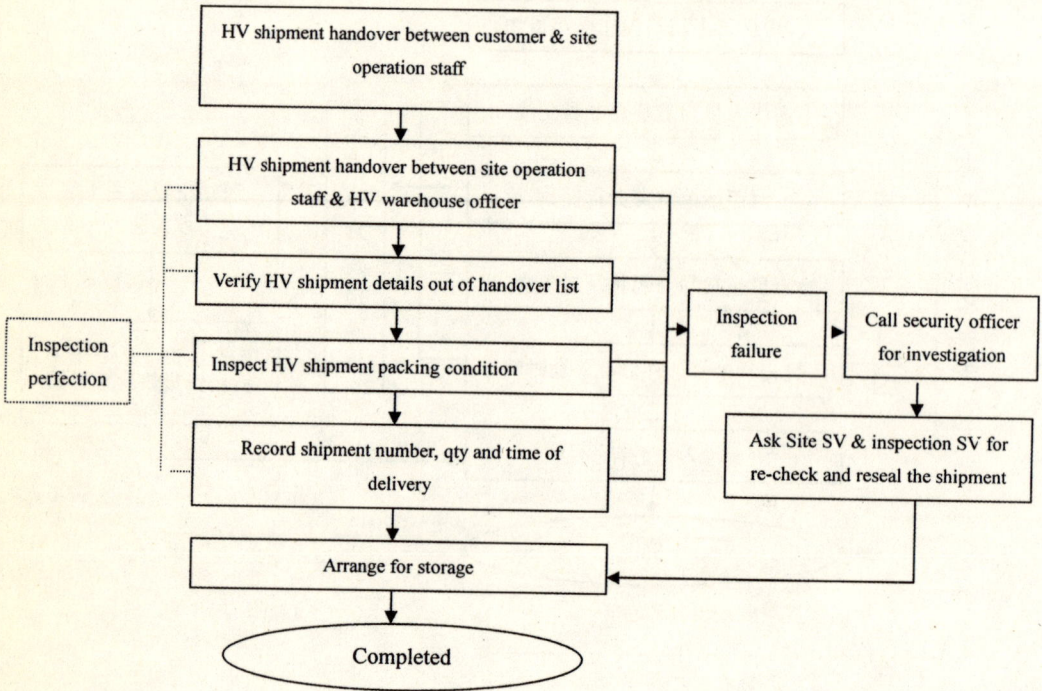

```
┌─────────────────────────────────────────┐
│ HV shipment handover between customer &  │
│           site operation staff           │
└─────────────────────────────────────────┘
                    │
                    ▼
┌─────────────────────────────────────────┐
│ HV shipment handover between site        │
│ operation staff & HV warehouse officer   │
└─────────────────────────────────────────┘
                    │
                    ▼
┌─────────────────────────────────────────┐
│ Verify HV shipment details out of        │
│ handover list                            │
└─────────────────────────────────────────┘
                    │
                    ▼
┌───────────────┐   ┌─────────────────────────────────────┐      ┌──────────────┐   ┌──────────────────┐
│  Inspection   │   │ Inspect HV shipment packing          │      │ Inspection   │   │ Call security    │
│  perfection   │   │ condition                            │─────▶│ failure      │──▶│ officer for      │
└───────────────┘   └─────────────────────────────────────┘      └──────────────┘   │ investigation    │
                    │                                                                 └──────────────────┘
                    ▼                                                                          │
┌─────────────────────────────────────────┐                      ┌────────────────────────────────────┐
│ Record shipment number, qty and time of  │                      │ Ask Site SV & inspection SV for      │
│ delivery                                  │                      │ re-check and reseal the shipment     │
└─────────────────────────────────────────┘                      └────────────────────────────────────┘
                    │                                                              │
                    ▼                                                              │
┌─────────────────────────────────────────┐◀──────────────────────────────────────┘
│            Arrange for storage            │
└─────────────────────────────────────────┘
                    │
                    ▼
          ╭───────────────────────╮
          │       Completed        │
          ╰───────────────────────╯
```

三、贵重货物出仓

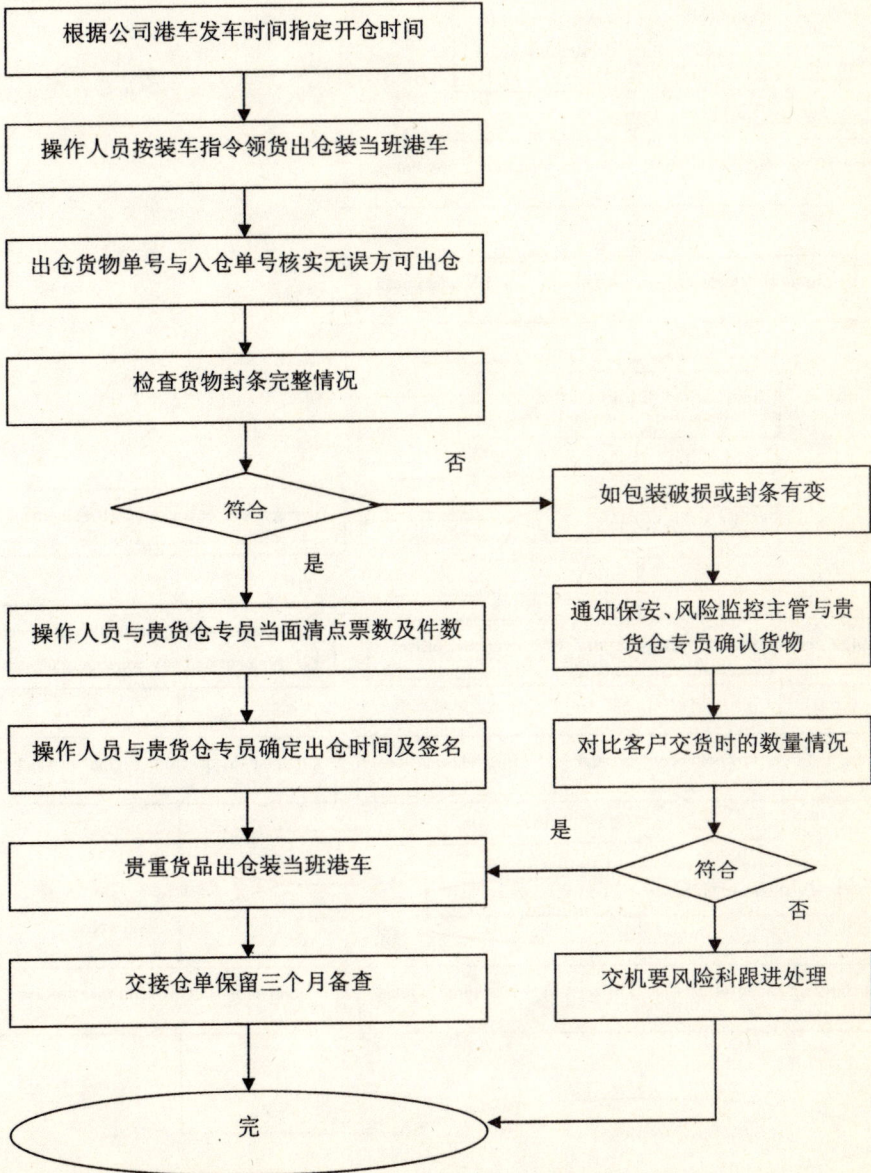

```
┌─────────────────────────────────┐
│  根据公司港车发车时间指定开仓时间  │
└─────────────────────────────────┘
                 ↓
┌─────────────────────────────────┐
│  操作人员按装车指令领货出仓装当班港车  │
└─────────────────────────────────┘
                 ↓
┌─────────────────────────────────┐
│  出仓货物单号与入仓单号核实无误方可出仓  │
└─────────────────────────────────┘
                 ↓
┌─────────────────────────────────┐
│       检查货物封条完整情况        │
└─────────────────────────────────┘
                 ↓
              ◇ 符合 ◇ ── 否 ──→ ┌──────────────────┐
                 │ 是              │  如包装破损或封条有变  │
                 ↓                 └──────────────────┘
┌────────────────────────┐                ↓
│ 操作人员与贵货仓专员当面清点票数及件数 │  ┌──────────────────────────┐
└────────────────────────┘        │ 通知保安、风险监控主管与贵货仓专员确认货物 │
                 ↓                 └──────────────────────────┘
┌────────────────────────┐                ↓
│ 操作人员与贵货仓专员确定出仓时间及签名 │  ┌──────────────────┐
└────────────────────────┘        │  对比客户交货时的数量情况  │
                 ↓                 └──────────────────┘
┌────────────────────┐                   ↓
│  贵重货品出仓装当班港车  │←── 是 ──── ◇ 符合 ◇
└────────────────────┘                   │ 否
                 ↓                        ↓
┌────────────────────┐       ┌──────────────────┐
│  交接仓单保留三个月备查  │       │  交机要风险科跟进处理  │
└────────────────────┘       └──────────────────┘
                 ↓                        │
             (  完  )←────────────────────┘
```

3. Take out HV Shipment Procedure

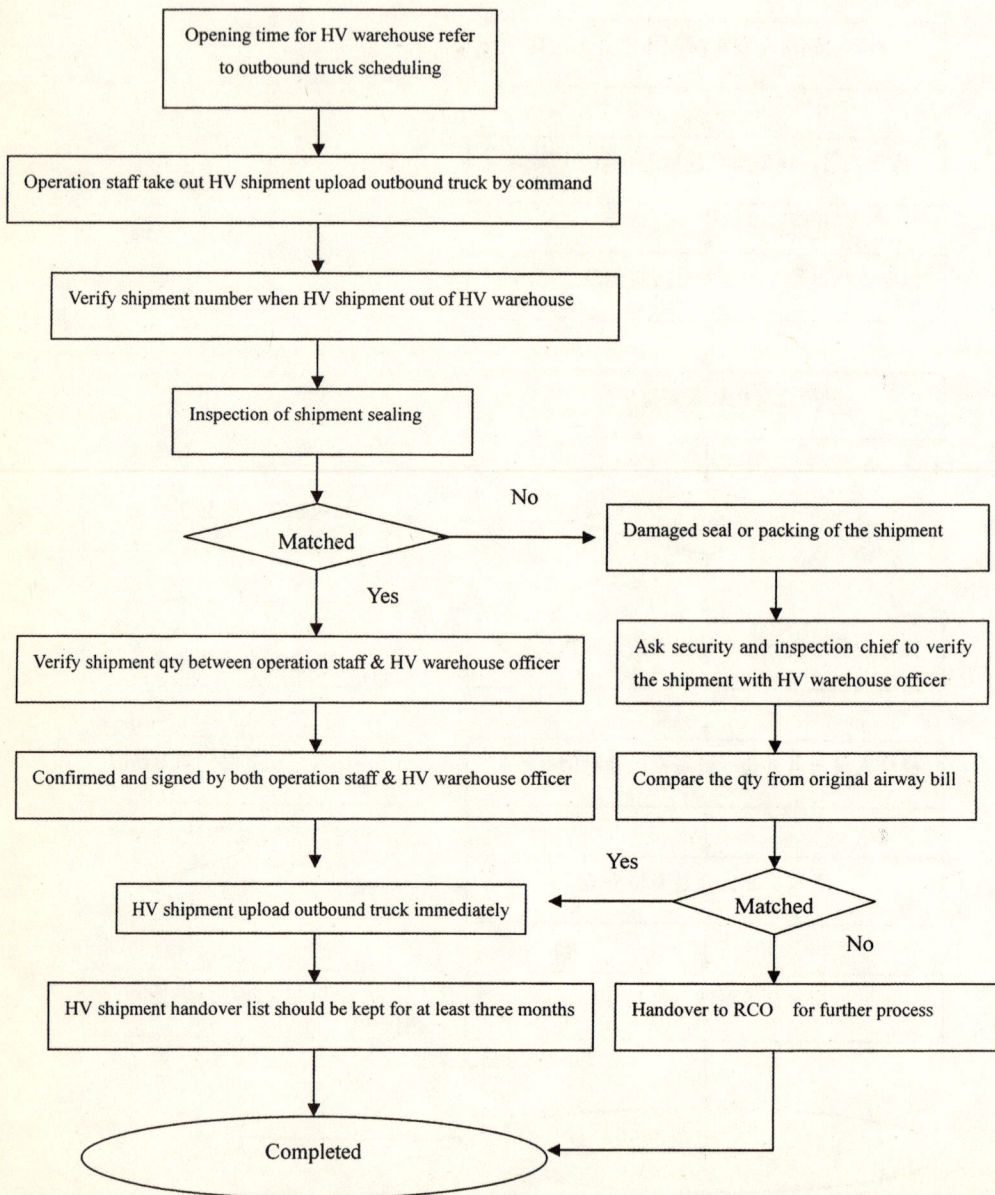

```
┌─────────────────────────────────────┐
│  Opening time for HV warehouse refer │
│     to outbound truck scheduling     │
└─────────────────────────────────────┘
                    │
                    ▼
┌──────────────────────────────────────────────────────────────┐
│ Operation staff take out HV shipment upload outbound truck by command │
└──────────────────────────────────────────────────────────────┘
                    │
                    ▼
┌──────────────────────────────────────────────────────────┐
│ Verify shipment number when HV shipment out of HV warehouse │
└──────────────────────────────────────────────────────────┘
                    │
                    ▼
┌─────────────────────────────────┐
│  Inspection of shipment sealing  │
└─────────────────────────────────┘
                    │
                    ▼
                                    No
              ◇ Matched ◇ ──────────────────▶ ┌──────────────────────────────────────┐
                    │                          │ Damaged seal or packing of the shipment │
                   Yes                         └──────────────────────────────────────┘
                    │                                         │
                    ▼                                         ▼
┌──────────────────────────────────────────────┐  ┌────────────────────────────────────────┐
│ Verify shipment qty between operation staff & │  │ Ask security and inspection chief to verify │
│          HV warehouse officer                  │  │ the shipment with HV warehouse officer     │
└──────────────────────────────────────────────┘  └────────────────────────────────────────┘
                    │                                         │
                    ▼                                         ▼
┌──────────────────────────────────────────────┐  ┌──────────────────────────────────────┐
│ Confirmed and signed by both operation staff  │  │ Compare the qty from original airway bill │
│          & HV warehouse officer                │  └──────────────────────────────────────┘
└──────────────────────────────────────────────┘              │
                    │                          Yes             ▼
                    ▼                     ◀────────── ◇ Matched ◇
┌──────────────────────────────────────────────┐              │
│ HV shipment upload outbound truck immediately  │             No
└──────────────────────────────────────────────┘              │
                    │                                          ▼
                    ▼                              ┌────────────────────────────────────┐
┌──────────────────────────────────────────────────────┐  │ Handover to RCO  for further process │
│ HV shipment handover list should be kept for at least  │  └────────────────────────────────────┘
│              three months                              │              │
└──────────────────────────────────────────────────────┘              │
                    │                                                  │
                    ▼                                                  │
              (    Completed    ) ◀──────────────────────────────────┘
```